Sojourn on the Bohemian Highway

Sojourn on the Bohemian Highway

by

Tomás Gayton

Poetic Matrix Press

Poetic Matrix Press
www.poeticmatrix.com

For my grandfather, John Thomas (J.T.) Gayton, whose escape from the Black Codes of Mississippi and move to the Pacific Northwest gave me the freedom to pursue my passion and to my mother, Emma, whose love sustained me on the open road.

Acknowledgements

I would like to thank those who worked patiently with me to produce this latest chapter of my life in verse, especially: Jennifer Woolm, Justin and Melissa Murray, John Peterson, Steve Kowit, J. Glenn and Barbara Evans for their review and helpful comments and Tyler Campbell for his cover design.

Muchisimas Gracias.

Contents

Author Biography

Travelin'

Travelin' in two directions
East and West
then
North and South

In a race against time
I don't know why
Nor do I care
When I arrive or where

Welcome, o life!
I go to encounter for the millionth time the reality of experience
and to forge in the smithy of my soul the uncreated
conscience of my race!

-James Joyce
A Portrait of the Artist as a Young Man

Afoot and light-hearted I take to the open road,
Healthy, free, the world before me,
The long brown path before me leading wherever I choose.

-Walt Whitman
Song of the Open Road

[Travel] is the pleasure of searching and the pleasure of an
adventure. You are nourishing something that's very important,
your dreams.

-Paulo Coelho
The Pilgrimage

Afro-Caribbean Muse

The Guest House on Tanca Street

I venture out into the world, this time the Caribbean, like a moth seeking a flame. I have no fixed itinerary except a vague idea that this trip, like all the others, will provide me enough adventure and inspiration to justify the effort.

In the morning the plane lands in Puerto Rico and I take a bus to Old San Juan. I get off at the bus terminal in the old city and haul my bag and myself up the street where I take the trolley that drops me off in front of The Guest House on Tanca Street.

My room is at the end of a long hallway in an old building in the heart of Old San Juan. From my bay window I see the back of a rustic red brick building. There is a bed with clean sheets, a fridge, a squeaky ceiling fan and a small but adequate closet—all the necessities of life. I unpack and leave to explore my new neighborhood.

After traversing the narrow streets and dodging tourists boarding cruise ships in the harbor, I find a quiet bar on San Sebastian and order a *cuba libre*. I sit at the mahogany bar sipping my rum & coke, watching an American pro-football game on the TV above the bar. You know you are in an American colony when the bars are filled with *gringos* watching pro-football games in real time on ESPN.

Old San Juan is a shopping mall for throngs of *turistas* flowing from the portal of floating cruise ship hotels. They crowd the streets during the day, peering into tourist shops and frequenting the many restaurants, bars and cafés lining the narrow streets and alleys in the old town. Again I am reminded of Puerto Rico's colonial status as I stroll the cobble-stoned streets past small shops selling seashells, bikinis, precious stones, and carnival masks, alongside the Starbucks, Burger King and McDonald's.

At night I discover el Callejón de la Capilla, the Chapel Alley, across from the chapel of San Francisco. In this urban alley graffiti shouts from its grey walls, "The white man is doomed, FBI

3

Asesinos *mataron el hombre pero no la idea*" (referring to the recent murder and suspected assassination of Puerto Rican nationalist leader Filiberto Ojeda Rios by the FBI).

On el Callejón I sit at a small café sipping my Bacardi and lime, watching the parade of swinging *señoritas* and cool cats who at midnight pass through the alley into the NuYoRican Club where *la música Latina, la rumba y salsa* resonate until the break of dawn when I return to my empty bed on a sloping street in old San Juan.

After exploring Old San Juan, I walk down the hall to my room and peek into the slightly open door of a room a couple doors up and across from mine. Inside I see a large painting of a lovely nude Asian woman hanging on the wall. The hotel owner, Señor Castro, says a Persian doctor has been living there for several years.

The next day I stop at doctor's slightly open door. Curiosity and a rash along my lower right cheek compel me to knock softly on it. A short stout man with an unshaven face and wild gray hair appears at the door. I introduce myself as his neighbor from down the hall and he invites me into his small studio apartment. He unfolds a chair and seats me next to a small cluttered round table. He sits across from me on his rumpled bed dangling his hairy twisted toes.

The floor is strewn with coffee grounds and cigarette butts. Beside Dr. Shah's bed is a Persian prayer rug. Dr. Shah says, "I can't read English although I speak it quite well and I can read Spanish but I can't speak it very well." He cooks his meals on a hot plate lying on the floor of his room. He smokes cigarettes, drinks beer and rum. He tells me about his life of close calls and conspiracies and shows me an old photo of him standing on the roof with a full head of black hair flexing bountiful biceps.

Dr. Shah treats my skin rash with a white cream he squeezes from a tube buried under empty wrappers and bread crumbs on the small table across from his bed. I ask him about the nude painting. "The Japanese girl is my ex-lover. She cost me a fortune and then she left me when the money ran out," he says ruefully as he scratches his toes. Dr. Shah sits on the edge of his bed talking in paranoiac riddles. He says "I hardly ever leave my room. I stay here and sometimes talk to travelers like you." The doctor says his health has been fragile since he survived an attempt on his life by a black guy who lives upstairs and a Jewish millionaire who lives in Tel Aviv. I thank him for treating my rash and offer him a beer, which he kindly accepts. On my way out he hands me his card.

Once a day during my stay in Old San Juan I interrupt the doctor's madcap meditations. He warmly welcomes me, unfolds a chair for me to sit, offers me a beer and fruit and we talk about his paranoid fantasies. On one occasion I rewrite, in English, a spiritually inspiring letter he's sending to a friend.

Damaras is my next door neighbor. She is a Santeria devotee and a Nuyorican with an attitude. She is also the local pot supplier. She gets her marijuana from La Perla, a downscale barrio that sits below the wall on the coastline not far from here. When sober she is very agreeable and loans me a tea cup. However, one day when I wander out onto the balcony overlooking the cobblestone street, Damaras is sitting there stoned on the balcony sipping her rum. Our casual conversation ends when she shouts at me, "Why do you ask so many questions?" I retreat into un-lawyer-like silence and let her ramble on into incoherence before I descend the stairway to the colorful colonial street scene below.

One night while lounging on the roof looking at the cruise ships on the harbor I meet mellow Jurriaan, the Flying Dutchman. He pilots a sloop and is on his six month vacation from cruising tourists on Holland's inland sea. He is long, lean and blond. We hang out together for a few days diggin' the scene on el Callejón, drinking rum and dancing the nights away at the NuYo Rican Café. Jurriaan is a firm believer in water therapy, "Water can cure anything. By drinking it, swimming in it and cleaning with it. It kills lots of harmful bacteria," he says earnestly.

On Christmas Eve, Jurriaan and I attend midnight mass at the Chapel of San Francisco then we join a few new friends on the roof of the Guest House on Tanca Street. We share the sacrament in the mystery of this star-studded night in Old San Juan. Jurriaan falls in love with a lovely New York dancer who has joined us in our rooftop reverie. After bidding them good night, I return to my room and fall into a blissful sleep.

On Christmas Day, I welcome Delores, an old flame from San Diego, to Old San Juan. I take her on a tour of the colony and introduce her to my new friends. After celebrating Christmas with Delores, Jurriaan and his New York girlfriend, I kiss Delores goodbye, and after the dogs sniff my bags, I get on the plane and take a night flight to the Dominican Republic.

Zona Colonial

I arrive in Santo Domingo at midnight, my flight having been delayed a couple hours by a mechanical problem. Bettye, the owner of la Galeria guest house, where I have a reservation, has arranged for Jesus to drive me to her place in la Zona Colonial on la Plaza Toledo.

I ride down *el malecón* and through the dusky streets of Santo Domingo until arriving in front of a two-story, red-tiled colonial style building facing a dark empty street. I have no pesos so I give Jesus dollars and he loans me some pesos. He gives me the key to my room and the key to the barred security gate. Jesus wishes me good night and takes off into the night. I have enough light from a distant street lamp to place the key in the lock to the wrought iron gate. As I try to unlock the gate a figure lunges at me from the shadows and collapses at my feet. After I recover from the shock I see a nondescript figure writhing on the ground. She or maybe he is begging for pesos. This poor soul extends a hand, I hurriedly hand over some pesos, open the door and escape into my room.

The next morning after shaving and showering, I walk out into the bright sunshine and onto the now bustling street. I walk around *la casa* onto la Plaza Toledo and into la Galería where I find buxom middle-aged blond Bettye, dressed in a flossy black satin lace

6

dress, showing a fine piece of Haitian art to a tourist. Bettye greets me warmly once her prospective client leaves. She and I sit in her gallery sipping tea while we catch up on each other's lives. She once lived in my old hometown, La Jolla, California. She says she has one of the finest collections of Dominican and Haitian art in the country. I give her a copy of my latest poetry book and she proposes that I do a reading in her gallery. I agree to after I return from my island tour.

While wandering in the upscale Zona Colonial at night I happen upon the Cuban Culture Club, a stone's throw from la Plaza de Cristobal Colón, where I sit down for dinner, order rum and drink in *el ritmo cubano*. After two days and nights exploring the cafés, jewelry stores and bars on Parque Colón, I head north to Sosúa and the beach.

Sosúa is a small town on the north coast between the resort towns of Puerto Plata and Cabarete. I drop off my gear at Rocky's Rock & Blues Bar Hotel and head for the nearby beach. I stroll the beach lined with funky bars and cafés filled with *Anglos* on holiday. The long stretch of beach is lined with European-owned and occupied bars, restaurants and shops selling t-shirts and sodas.

At night I venture out with Alban and Sarah, a young couple from Los Angeles whom I met in the guest house while using the internet. Alban is a French national living and working in Los Angeles. Sarah is his Eurasian American fiancée. She's employed by the Museum of Latin American Art in Long Beach, California.

We stroll around the darkened neighborhood where Christmas decorations compete with neon lights, until we stop at a huge oblong open-air bar. The place is jumpin' with bright lights and scantily clad girls flitting like butterflies from bar stool to bar stool seeking the nectar of the night from money-laden middle-aged tourists sitting at the bar. My new friends and I circle the bar then walk up the arcing stairway to the upper bar and dance floor that is virtually empty. We order drinks and sit at a cocktail table peering down through Plexiglas on the denizens of the lower bar flirting, drinking and philandering through the Dominican night. After a while the voyeurism loses its charm and we leave behind the hordes of hookers and the legion of lusting gringos. I say good night to Alban and Sarah and start to cross the road to my room in the guesthouse.

Then I hear the voice of a deranged angel of the night. I see her across the street just before she makes a beeline for me shouting, "Are you looking for a date? Can I make you happy?" I keep on walking as she catches up with me, then lunges at me and grabs my crotch. Startled, I rush back to the hotel and lock my door.

I leave this brothel by the bay the very next day on a cross-island bus ride to Las Galeras, a tiny quiet tourist town on the far northeast coast of La Samaná peninsula. Here I discover *la cultura dominicana y el ritmo dominicano*, where the sea's horizon is a blend of heavenly hues of blue.

I check into el Paradiso Bungalow situated on the beach near the town center. This is a quiet and laid-back place where tourists don't congest the streets but swim and sun on the beach and eat and drink in their hotels. There are a few small restaurants and bars near the intersection, but most socializing occurs at the tourist hotels and at the open air bar and restaurant located at the end of the main street on the beach front where locals outnumber *los turistas*. Here everyone chills on soulful seafood washed down with rum and beer. The scene is mellow and the European ex-pats are well adjusted to the beach culture and idyllic scenery. The sunsets are postcard-perfect on the turquoise sea.

I attend a New Year's Eve party on the remote and romantic beach at El Rincón. We welcome the New Year with rum and lobster under a panoply of sparkling stars and moon shine on the obsidian sea. Lovely ladies teach me La Bachata to Afro-Dominicano rhythms played by an inspired ensemble of local musicians.

Baile La Bachata

Bonita señorita cuánto cobras
por enseñarme a bailar
La bachata?

"Don Tomás, nada para ti"

Uno dos tres cuatro
Adelante atrás a un lado
Uno dos tres cuatro
Adelante atras a un lado

Bonita morena muchas gracias
Para enseñarme
A bailar la bachata

Uno dos tres cuatro
Adelante atrás a un lado
Uno dos tres cuatro
Adelante atrás a un lado

Ahora bonita señorita
Puedes enseñarme sobre el amor

"No más que la bachata don Tomás"

Uno dos tres cuatro
Adelante atrás a un lado
Uno dos tres cuatro
Adelante atras a un lado

After several days strolling the idyllic beaches and swimming in the warm sea, I depart from this tranquil spot on God's good earth for Las Terranas, a city situated on the north coast of La Samaná peninsula.

9

While waiting at the hotel bar for a *concho* (pickups and minivans converted to public transport) to Samaná, I meet Sam, local tour guide from southern Asia. I buy him a beer and we talk. For a modest price, he offers to take me on a nature tour of the island. I decline his offer and ask him if he is a Muslim.

Smiling he says, "I am a Muslim when it relates to women and Catholic when it relates to drinking." We laugh and while the time away until the *concho* stops in front of the bar. I say goodbye to Sam and Las Galeras heading west on the open road.

La Luna

La Luna is wise and understanding
so when I'm on the open road
I talk to the moon to sort out
life's countless complexities
Tonight I'm confessing to the moon
how lonely life is without love
She beams down on me and whispers in my ear
"Never fear my son, La Luna loves you"

On the ride from tranquil Las Galeras to Las Terrenas, I am sitting in the back of a pickup on a wooden bench with a load of locals who climb on and jump off at each stop in each small town or village. Midway across the peninsula the driver stops and a good-looking brown skinned young man climbs onto the back and sits on a bench facing me.

He has a grotesquely swollen scarred forearm. He sees my pained expression and introduces himself to me as we careen down the narrow road across the island nation. Antonio tells me how he crushed his forearm in a *motoconcho* (motorbike) accident. After several surgeries he has been left with a forearm filled with fragments of bone floating in a mass of blood clots and severed veins. Antonio lives in constant low grade pain. He has no sling to carry his burden. He bravely holds it up, a stark reminder of human frailty and strength. The life of this smiling young man has been shattered like the bone in his forearm.

Wishfully, I tell him to go to neighboring Cuba where they have excellent surgeons who are affordable. Still smiling he says he cannot afford the plane fare. He jumps off just outside of Las Terrenas. He has an appointment with another Dominican doctor who he hopes can heal his fractured future.

Paradise is afflicted by a cacophony of *motoconchos* racing up and down *el malecón* and a plethora of European expats who own most of the hotels, restaurants and shops. I must say the whites have adjusted well to life in this laid back beach town. They seem to have everything under control, including the locals.

The main road along the waterfront is where the action is: outdoor restaurants, bars, discos and other tourist attractions. My favorite venues are the Haitian art galleries with the Haitian artists sitting before canvases with paint and brush. I buy a couple pieces of Haitian art from street vendors on my way through town to the barrio where the amiable hostess of a locally owned restaurant serves up tasty home-cooked meals and cool beer. One day while eating at a café bar on the beach a local shares with me a popular joke on *la isla turistica*:

> *How does one identify a Frenchman in the Dominican Republic?*
> *He has a baguette in one hand and a dominicana in the other.*
> *How does one recognize a German in the Dominican Republic?*
> *He has a beer in one hand and a dominicana in the other.*
> *How does one know an Italian in the Dominican Republic?*
> *He has a dominicana in each hand.*

I meet the cordial middle-aged French woman, Monique, who owns the café. We discuss the Dominican scene and people. Monique believes, "The Dominicans have no culture." Caught by surprise I ask, "What do you mean by that?" She says, "They don't have any sense of national or racial pride."

National pride when taken to an extreme can result in xenophobic Neo-Con Nationalism. However, Monique makes a poignant point when it comes to the absence of racial pride. Like most Latin Americans, Dominicans suffer from pigmentocracy. They distinguish degrees of negritude with lighter complexions preferred and privileged. Darker complexions are despised and deprived. The upper class and virtually all of the campaign posters that line the roads and towns clearly define who rules this island—the high yellas and near whites. Unlike Haitians and Cubans, they are reticent about acknowledging their African ancestry, culture and traditions. They would rather be called "Indios," than Afro-Latinos.

My next stop after a long ride in a cramped *concho* is Santiago, the second city of La Republica Dominicana nestled below the island's verdant central highlands. I arrive in the rush of midday and take a taxi to a small hotel near the central plaza. When I arrive, slender and comely Dulkin is cleaning rooms. She drops everything and leads me to a room on the upper floor of this quaint two- story building. After I settle in my room and take a shower, Dulkin invites me to her mother's home for lunch.

It's a short walk from my hotel across a busy thoroughfare to where her mother and two sisters live. Her mother, Carmen, is a warm and hospitable middle-aged woman, darker complexioned than her three daughters. Carmen makes me feel right at home. She serves me a typical Dominican meal of *guandules* (green pigeon peas), *arroz y pollo con vino tinto*. Afterwards, sister Soccoro serves me superb dark Dominican rum and I recite some of my *poemas* in Spanish and give them a copy of my recently published bilingual poetry book of verse, *Vientos de Cambio*. They are very grateful and I leave feeling, for the first time, a close connection to the people of this *isla turistica*.

Carmen's other daughter, Theresa, is a government lawyer. Three single women and one child living in this comfortable two- story apartment in the heart of Santiago. I wonder as I walk back to my hotel room, where are the men in these women's lives?

One afternoon I climb the Monumento a los Héroes de la Restauración de la República where I enjoy the scenic view of the city and surrounding green-covered mountains. When I return to the hotel, three fellow *Colombiano* guests are gathered on the patio celebrating with loud talk, Latin music and rum. They invite me to join them. We engage in light-hearted conversation and drink rum and soda. They introduce me to their Dominican girlfriends who sit quietly sipping rum and giggling at the antics of their intoxicated patrons. Enrique, who appears to be the oldest, refuses to learn English because he hates *yanquis*. I remind him that the *yanquis* are propping up Colombia's right wing government. He shrugs and takes another shot of rum and soda.

The highlight of my trip to Santiago is my visit to el Museo Folkórico where noted Domincan poet Don Tomás Morel's son, Tomás Jr., is the curator. The museum is down a few blocks and around the corner from my hotel. Tomás gives me a tour of the museum with its folk art, Carnival *caretas* (masks) and costumes. The next day Tomás introduces me to a few of the local poets and we exchange poetry over rum and insightful conversation about the challenges of life in the Dominican Republic. On a wall of the museum I read a poignant quote from Don Tomás: *El hombre soltero vive como un rey Pero muere como un perro* (A single man lives like a king But dies like a dog).

One night I take a cab uptown to a club called Bar Code on Calle de Cuba. In this indoor/outdoor restaurant bar the locals gather to dance the night away to Afro-Dominican rhythms played by el Barco de Jazz Combo replete with *congas, bongos, tambores, guitarras y piano*. The guys and gals get down to the beat on the crowded dance floor.

In Santiago, I become close to the culture of the Dominican Republic. Here, I can converse with locals and walk the streets without being attacked by desperate hookers. Here one finds authentic Dominican art in the galleries and best of all there is hardly a *gringo* anywhere to be seen.

Tragically, the life of Haitians living in the Dominican Republic is more perilous than that of the undocumented Latinos living in the United States. It is estimated that one million Haitians live in the DR with only a few thousand living here legally, about the same number of Dominicans live in the USA. Most of the Haitians I see are artists in the numerous galleries lining the streets of tourist towns like las Terranas. The majority of Haitians live in the shadows and on the side streets as they struggle to survive doing jobs the Dominicans won't do. The next morning I am on my way south returning to Santo Domingo and then home.

I arrive by taxi at la Zona Colonial on Thursday in the early afternoon and rent a room in the Hotel Freeman on Calle Isabel La Católica near Parque Colón only a few doors from my first home in the Dominican Republic. After settling in, I walk down the street to Bettye's Galleria. She warmly welcomes me home and confirms my poetry reading on Saturday.

On Friday the 13th I taxi to the Museo de Arte Morderna near the center of the city. Highlights of the Museo del Hombre Dominicano include a collection of Taíno artifacts, a section on slavery during the colonial period and African influences in the Dominican Republic, including a section dedicated to *vodun* (voodoo). After viewing the permanent collection of Dominican art at the Museo de Arte Moderno, I cross a busy street to catch a *concho* to the Zona Colonial.

I see folks lined up in front of a grey nondescript one-story building. I pull out my camera to take a photo of this colorful group of Dominicans. After snapping the photo I hear a loud authoritative voice behind me. I turn and see a tall black Dominican soldier standing in the shade beside the building gesturing for me to approach him. Puzzled, I ask him in Spanish, "*Que quieres?*" "What do you want?" He ignores my question and orders me to enter the area where he stands, an area cordoned by a steel cable connected to concrete pylons. I reluctantly enter the area and again ask him, "*Que quieres? Porque me* llamó?" "Why did you call me?" He sternly asks to see my film. I ask him, "*Por que.*" He tells me it is forbidden to take photos. I ask him, "*Por que.*" He starts rattling off in clipped Spanish about it being forbidden to take photos of this building. I know I am in deep shit when he insists on taking my film. I refuse. Just as the soldier and I reach the tipping point in our standoff, a *mulato* man in civilian clothes wearing an official ID on a necklace arrives on the scene. He tells me in English, "It is forbidden to take photos of the American consulate."

"Since when?" I ask.

"Since 9-11," he replies.

I tell him, "I had no idea this was the American Consulate. There is nothing indicating that this is the American Consulate. There is no American flag or signs forbidding the taking of photos, *nada.*" I explain that I'm a black American taking photos for artistic reasons to capture a cross section of Dominican faces.

With a smile the *mulato* says, "Tomás, here you are white. These people are in line to obtain visas to the U.S.A." He says, "The soldier is just doing his job. Just go along with the officer."

I follow his advice and give the soldier my driver's license. The soldier takes it and disappears into the building. He returns after a short while. He is holding a clip board. It's an incident report. After questioning me about who I am and where I come from, he mellows and hands me my license. I hail the first taxi I see and head back to the hotel. A close call on Friday the 13th.

Saturday afternoon Bettye provides an abundance of fine wine and finger food for the guests who attend my poetry reading in her Galleria. My words are warmly received by the many American expats in attendance and by César Zapata, the Secretario de Cultura. I give him an autographed copy of *Vientos.* He invites me to be a guest on his radio talk show. I regrettably decline his invitation due to my scheduled departure early Sunday morning.

Afro-Colombia

Atardecer en Taganga

*There is no hurry here
only* el ritmo *Afro-Caribe
and the tropical winds
swaying* las palmas
*sweeping away
the losses of yesterday
as I wait under a full moon
for sunrise
on a beach by the bay*

Mulatania

*I'm savoring the land of chocolate & honey
where ripe mangoes bounce
in bikinis strolling on sand
and in skin tight jeans
on the cobblestone streets
of colonial Cartagena*

Café Havana

*At midnite the band begins to play
and all the tables fill as*
el ritmo *inspires my feet to move
to* la salsa y la cumbia *beat
blissfully swingin'
with my brothers and sisters
in the café and on the street
as* la madrugada *arrives
Cartagena finally falls asleep*

Ciudad Perdida (Lost City)

I'm hiking the Sierra Nevada
into the hidden lost city
where the Tayrona and Arhuaco
tribal spirits reside
on stone walls
paths, terraces, in thatched huts
y las hamacas

The Madoffs have it all wrong:
concrete, paper and plastic
fast cars, private clubs
and con games can't compensate
for lost buffalo, tom tom
tepee and tomahawk

Plaza de la Trinidad

I wander up the shadowy street
at sunset and find families
who fill the plaza
with laughter and song

I watch children hanging
on open arms of stone saints
before a colonial church
jumping on trampolines
zooming on skateboards
doing handstands and cart wheeling
over and under rumba rhythms

Kuna Yala

San Blas Quinceañera

At midnight
I swing on mi hamaca
en mi cabaña *as*
Kuna Yala angels of light
sparkle and dance
in the heavens above
and virgins celebrate
by cutting their raven hair—
wrapping colorful beads
around tender brown calves—
wearing rainbow blouses
and hand woven scarves

While the men drink
sing, stagger and sway
all night and all day

Arco Iris

Today at noon on the road
from San Blas to Panama City
the jeep driver's teenage son
looks at the sky and shouts
"Mira! Mira!"

I wonder what has moved this boy
who laid silent on his back
as we bumped over la cordillera*?*

Then the jeep stops and we jump out
to witness a rainbow halo the sun

Atardecer en Panamá

Leaning on the railing in Luna's Castle
at sundown
watching black winged Talingos circle above
and kids of color kicking soccer balls
on cobblestone streets
as shadows spread
across the bay and up la rampa
the curtain falls on another day
in creaky colonial Casco Viejo
where the legacy of slavery is found
on weary faces walking the streets
and smiling faces selling fish in El Mercado

El Mercado de Mariscos

Panama has ships cruising the canal
as Colombian putas *enticingly smile at*
gringos *living behind high walls*
and Chinese touristas *crowding casinos*

But for me it's the ceviche y corvina
el chupe de camarones
y la sopa de mariscos
that satisfies my appetite

El Ritmo Cubano

i

Whether I'm sitting in Teatro Heredia
in Santiago at sundown
savoring my mojito and puffing a Cohiba
diggin' Danzon, Bolero y Son
or at club la Zorra y el Cuervo
in el Vedado at midnight
sipping my Havana Club
diggin' Afro-Cuban Jazz
I celebrate the Yoruba rites
of rum rhythm y rumba

ii

In Vedado lovely senoritas
of summer swing and sway
ripe mangoes and melons
as they stroll in style
down calle San Lazaro
to El Malecón at sunset
where mellow machismo
struts and swaggers
in sleeveless shirts
and lingering laughter
to the beat of the breaking waves
and rolling thunder

I finish my mojito
and join the throng
celebrating at sundown
the rites of rum
and Yoruba rumba
rumba rhythm

Mulata Melodia

*The blacks and whites may not love each other but they love las
mulatas and las mulatas love them.*

In Cuba you can't smoke reefer but you can drink rum anywhere anytime
except at meetings of the Central Committee when Fidel is presiding

You can't bring a Cuban woman to your hotel room but you can bring
as many as you want to your *casa particular*

Havana is a factory that turns out beautiful women of every chocolate
flavor and every honey hue

Sexy girls strut and sway in an unaffected way down busy boulevards
and avenues in tight jeans and minis into a salsa night of fun and play

Maria, holding a tan-colored fan, smiles as I sip my mojito gazing past
the swinging doors of Bar Monserrate to el Parque in Old Havana

Smittened by her smile I want to pierce her precious soul with mine
I want to kiss her luscious lips and touch her delicate finger tips

I want to caress and consume her delicious curves and contours
      I want her!

It's another hot and humid evening in Central Havana when she
arrives at *mi nido de amor via bici-taxi*

After dining and wining she sits at my table and tells me she is bored
with Benny Moré on the radio singing *"Te Quedaras" y "Oh! Vida"*

We move into my bedroom with the fan rotating above as I remove
her clothes and taste her tart papaya tongue and ripe mangos

As we sink into each other she whispers in my ear, "Where is the
condom? I have to go soon, where is the condom? I have to go"

Jinetera Holiday

i

It's January in Havana in bar Montserrat
festooned by *rosas y gladiolas*
The band serenades con *salsa y baladas*
cigar smoking, rum drinking *habaneros*
y gringos at honey colored sundown

Frenchman Frank laments how he met her
here last night, "She was stunning
in her spandex and tennis shoes
I saved her from the police
I gave her a night of pleasure
but I will never pay for sex again"
    So he says

Carlos is with Yaumara, the chocolate treat
he met on the street while looking for food
Her dark eyes are melancholy like Billy Holiday's
the tragic *negrita flacita con la bella culita*

Melissa walks in at midnight wearing black
stylish spike heels and a black leather jacket—
vampire to the bone—
She's got a hot date with a gringo and she's dressed to kill
  "When she bites you bleed $ $ $"

Stephanie from Santiago smiles and I'm hers
as she rides me from one high to another
to the rhythm of *congas y claves*
until half past the hour *del sol*

In *la manana* she leaves a note on my pillow:

Bueno mi amor yo quiero expresar que me siento muy bien que paso una noche maravillosa junto a ti y que estoy muy contenta de haber conocido un persona tan dulce y bueno y espero que esto no haya sido un pasatiempo.

ii

We meet María on the patio by *la catedral*
with her wide ebony eyes, curious and alive
an ivory smile and so smooth cinnamon skin

We invite her to join us on the patio
where we drink mojitos as
the band plays *rumbas y mambos*
and time stands still in Habana Vieja

where women wearing colored scarves
warmly greet each other as sandals scrape scraps
of cardboard set before open doors

iii

Angels weep *lágrima negras* on Santa Clara's
memorial shrine to Ernesto Che Guevara
Martyr Man of La Mancha
Hasta la Victoria Siempre Comandante!

At nightfall I meet the virgin of Santa Clara
wearing a mini-skirt and chewing gum—

We dance to Montanez's *Un Montón de Estrellas:*
Porque yo en el amor soy un idiota que he sufrido un mil derrotas/ que no tengo fuerza para defenderme/Pero ella casi siempre me aprovecha unas veces me desprecia y otras veces lo hace para entretenerme y es así.

*(Why am I such a fool in love who has suffered a thousand defeats.
Who doesn't have strength to defend myself. But she almost always
takes advantage of me and sometimes she scorns me and other times
she does it to entertain me and that's the way it is.)*

She says she wants to know me
She's surreal until she asks for money

iv

Standing alone on the hill overlooking Holguien
where *chicas* are forbidden to meet gringos
by day, but liaison in the darkness anyway

En la casa de música bronze black bellies & behinds
undulate *al ritmo* Cubano, striking a flame
in gyrating thighs. Lost in a tropical trance I shout—
Hola chica! si tu cocinas como tu caminas yo me como hasta la raspa
(If you cook like you walk I will eat the leftovers)
que bella las chicas, las mulattas, las trigueñas y morenas

Does El Abuelo see the children of the Revolution
Selling themselves to save the Revolution?

Safari Songs

Capetown

I arrive in Capetown in mid-December and settle into the Ashanti Lodge in the Garden District, my home away from home. The Ashanti Lodge is an old colonial mansion nestled at the foot of the steep southern sandstone slope of Table Mountain. The Lodge is a tiny intersection where I meet travelers seeking refuge from the chill of European winter and volunteers working for NGOs in the fields of education, HIV/AIDS prevention and treatment. We sit in the lodge's congenial Kumasi café sipping rooibos as white clouds cross the summit of Table Mountain driven by whistling southeasterly winds then spill over the edge in ethereal billowing beauty.

Capetown is a modern cosmopolitan city on the southern tip of Africa. However, ten years after apartheid was abolished and Nelson Mandela was elected president, the country is as before. Whites own most of the businesses and neighboring vineyards and farms. Many live in luxurious houses in the hills while black folks toil in their kitchens and homes. Except for the fortunate few who hold jobs in the government, most Blacks till the soil and live in the poor townships surrounding the thriving big cities. The ubiquitous Mercedes and BMWs seen on the streets of downtown Capetown are driven by whites not blacks and I see few blacks visit downtown Capetown at night or during the day.

It's a short walk from the Garden District to Long Street in the heart of Capetown's funky downtown. There I buy a spicy shawarma sandwich on my way to Mama Africa, the popular restaurant and night club, where a Congolese band is playing a mesmerizing medley of bebop and reggae rhythms to a jumpin' interracial crowd.

My new found friends from the Lodge attend my poetry reading at Capetown's Off Moroka Café Africaine on Adderley Street. The event is well attended by local white, colored (mixed race) and black South Africans. Richard Ishmail is the owner of the café which is one of the few non-white owned businesses in

Capetown. Thanks to the Ashanti's travel staff and amiable owner, Lisa Mason, I am able to visit many local sites not on the travel guides. Lisa also runs a foundation that provides aid to children living in the townships.

I visit District 6 on the West Cape where between 1968 and 1982 the Colored community of over 60,000 was forcibly evicted, their dwellings destroyed and moved to the West Cape flatlands some 25 kilometers away. Then I visit the townships in the flatlands to see how Capetown's Black and Colored communities are surviving after apartheid.

The teeming townships on the outskirts of South Africa's major cities are home to millions of poor Black families crammed into small iron sheeted cubicles waiting hopefully for education, jobs and a better life. However, the patience of Black and Colored youth is wearing thin. The Black masses anticipated a rapid improvement in their standard of living after the overthrow of apartheid. Unfortunately, the change in government has not resulted in a rapid transformation of the socio-economic status quo. The townships are growing increasingly restive and it will take a greater redistribution of wealth from top to bottom to avoid serious social conflict in the future.

One lovely day I hike up the arduous rocky trail to the summit of Table Mountain. Here I am on top of the world with a sunny view of Capetown, the coast and the sea. After trekking and trippin' on top of Table Mountain, I witness the flaming sun sink into the obsidian sea.

The next day I make the mandatory pilgrimage to Robben Island. A tear runs down my cheek onto the stone prison yard as I grip the bars of Nelson Mandela's former tiny prison cell and ponder how he survived 18 years in this cold drafty concrete cell sleeping on a mat with a woolen blanket. The Nobel Peace Prize winner transcended his twenty-seven years of captivity and suffering to lead his nation on the path of penance and reconciliation. Nelson Mandela is the sun whose gravity holds the disparate elements of South African society in peaceful orbit.

Mantra to Nelson Rolihlahla Mandela

Mandela broke the chain
Mandela was not broken

27 years of fearsome time alone
cold showers in winter
breaking a mountain of rock
on Robben Island

while Winnie and the children waited
with the wrath of apartheid

Mandela broke the chain
Mandela was not broken

70 years of struggle in
the streets of Soweto
where passive resistance met
bullets and blood
Invoking laws of God
he raised his fist

UMKONTO WE SIZWE
(spear of the nation)

Mandela broke the chain
Mandela was not broken

In early morning I drive up the Eastern Cape past Port Elizabeth to the idyllic coastal town of Knysna, where tourists and wealthy Whites dig the scene on the harbor with its internet cafés, fantastic art galleries and seafood restaurants. Here I consume oysters, mussels, calamari and saffron rice washed down with fine white wine. After feasting I take a short walk to Judah Square and wander around the outdoor market place until I meet a Rasta named Robert who invites me to his home in the hills. I accept Robert's invitation to visit his home in the Rasta colony on the hill above the city. When we arrive he introduces me to his fellow Rastafarians and shows me the sacred Rasta gathering place.

We walk to his house where I meet his white wife and their two lovely young daughters who playfully scurry through the house while we sit outside on his wooden deck, share the sacrament of love and groove on the reggae *djimba* beat played by the brethren who worship in Jah's holy temple overlooking tall green plots of *dagga* plants and the sea. Robert's words interrupt my meditation, "Like one love experience for the brethren too hung up on Hip Hop, Africa is calling you home."

My next stop is the northern coastal town of Transkei, Nelson Mandela's birthplace and the heartland of the Xhosa people. I drive through the small port town of East London passing a statue of anti-apartheid martyr, Steve Biko standing in front of City Hall with his hand extended in a gesture of peace and reconciliation.

In Mpande, Transkei I move into a rustic cabin in the Kraal, resting on a cliff, overlooking the Indian Ocean. After settling in, I'm invited to a Songoma ceremony celebrated with big bass drums and other percussion in a traditional round thatched hut. The female shaman dances barefoot while performing rituals and offering fire and incense to the ancestral spirits. We end the evening dancing with the shaman and local folks then walk on a muddy road back to the Kraal where we sit in the cliff side cabin, light up the sacrament and commune with our ancestral spirits.

Namibian Desert

In the late afternoon I board the overnight bus from Capetown to Windhoek, capital of the desert nation Namibia. The seat next to me is empty so I stretch out and look forward to catching up on my sleep after sundown. But just before the bus leaves the station, a blond, blue-eyed, young lady arrives and asks if she can take the empty seat. "Yes, sure you can."

During our night ride sharing small talk and music, German Sagittarian Alexandra and I agree to share a room at the Chameleon Lodge in Windhoek. Over breakfast the next morning we agree to travel Namibia together. We spend Christmas Eve and Christmas Day touring the pleasant and hospitable capital city of Windhoek. I rent a small Japanese car and Alex agrees to drive because I don't feel safe driving with the steering wheel on the passenger side.

We travel east to the Atlantic coastal town of Swakopmund. After a chilly night in a cozy B&B we head south along the coast passing huge sand dunes crowded with white youth surfing, sledding and skiing the powdery slopes.

We arrive at the single-story lodge, Solitaire, a lonely outpost on the west coast of the vast Namibian desert. The sun hovers in the western sky as streaks of gold stretch across the desiccated landscape. Several White guests are diving and splashing in the swimming pool as we carry our bags to our room on the northwest corner of the quad. The room is huge with a double bed bearing a faux leopard skin cover. I hold out hope that we could achieve a harmonious connection on the leopard skin.

After settling in our room, we set out on what I hope is a romantic sunset stroll in the desert. We walk together for a while and suddenly, she says, "I want to be alone."

Surprised, I say, "*Adios*," and head up a steep rise followed by a small stray dog with a wagging tail that has tagged along during our walk. I watch the amber lantern sink slowly into the blue horizon.

I return to the lodge after sundown just as the final sliver of light is lost in a silent sea of desert sand. I walk over to the lighted patio where White guests are dining and sipping wine at small tables. An amiable young couple from South Africa invites me to join them.

As the darkness deepens around the patio, my anxiety deepens for the wild one who has not returned from her stroll in the desert. A young fellow wearing a white chef's outfit joins us on the patio. He sits across from me and asks, "Are you a writer?"

"Yes," I reply.

"Well!" he says, "I just want you to know that I hate America."

Nonplussed and taken by surprise I say, "No worries, I consider myself a citizen of the world." That doesn't resonate with this young American hater. Before I can provide my antagonist with reasons why he should not hate America, Alex appears out of the darkness. I see her and say, "Hey girl! I was beginning to worry about you." Silently, she joins us and orders a glass of wine.

Alex seems anxious and agitated as she sips her red wine. She ignores me and gets into a deep conversation in German with the anti-American chef.

As midnight approaches I finish my wine and excuse myself. I stop by the store and talk to the middle aged burly Afrikaner behind the counter, who asks me, "Where are you from?" I tell him I am from California. He says, "Oh! So you're an American are ya! You know George Bush is a Jew don't ya?" I'm stunned into silence by this crazed outburst from this otherwise amiable fellow. As I bid adieu and head for the door he shouts, "Bush is the head of a Zionist conspiracy to take over the world!" Exhausted, I drift across the cloister to my room and crash. As I doze off, I remember we have a 4:00 AM wakeup call in order to arrive at the Namib dunes of Sossussvlei by sunrise.

I am fast asleep when the wild woman walks in, turns on the lights and wakens me. Alex roams around at midnight smoking a cig and bobbing to tunes on her Walkman. I freak out and shout, "Go to bed or get out!" She grabs her sleeping bag and stalks out of the room without turning off the light. I get up to shut off the lights and lock the door. She spends the night somewhere. I assume she is sleeping with the anti-American chef.

Before sunrise I hear a knock at my door. It's Alex. I don't move. I have decided not to go any farther with her. I refuse to answer the door. She starts pounding on the door and shouting my name. "Tomás, open the door!" Furious, she marches around the complex and shouts through the closed shutters, "Tomás wake up! We have to go!" I figure she must have awakened everyone with her histrionics, but I don't care. I just want to waken from this nightmare and resume a life without Alex.

Then I hear a key in the lock and she enters the room totally frazzled but more subdued. She apologizes for freaking out and we are on the road again with Alex driving like Mad Max through the Namib Desert Park on a narrow two lane road with frequent rises that make it difficult to see oncoming traffic.

I implore Alex to slow down but she refuses. She insists, "This is the only way I know how to drive." She grows increasingly perturbed with my protestations and calls me a coward as she steps on the gas. I grab under the car seat with both hands in a futile effort to achieve some slight sense of security. After a race through the desert we arrive at the entrance to Sossussvlei Park. The park ranger issues a day permit, gives us the rules then lifts the guardrail and we pass into the silence of the dunes.

After a breathtaking ride through landscapes of sand rising in stark steep ridges and soft sloping mounds, we park the car and hike on the dunes leaving footprints behind us. Vast stretches of soft silky sand rise in sharp smooth formations as far as the eye can see. I strip on the summit of a sand dune basking under the bright sun, gazing into the crystal blue sky.

Naked, I stand, arms raised on the summit of a dune, stunned by the silence of steep sloping sand. In the heat of noon we leave the dunes heading southeast across the Namib Desert to the Kalahari.

Alex resumes her Red Baroness routine on the narrow gravel roads of the Namib Desert. She refuses to slow down, driving full speed with one hand on the wheel and the other on a road map while I desperately hold on to the car seat and pray.

> *I'm riding on the white highway*
> *with the Red Baroness*
> *across the cumin-colored Kalahari*
> *into the blue sky*
> *where San people leave no tracks*
> *and there is no traffic*
> *only the whisper of the wind*
> *on surface of sand*

After hours on the road traversing Namibia's striking landscape we arrive at sunset in Cochas, a small town on the western edge of the Kalahari near the Botswana border.

We rent a room that opens to a patio, bar and pool in a quaint colonial hotel. We collapse on separate beds. I'm exhausted and frustrated with her driving. Alex grows increasingly irascible as I grow increasingly frustrated by her reckless driving. But she knows I need her to drive, even to the ends of the earth and over the edge.

The next day, we stroll the paprika-powdered Kalihari with its flourishing desert flora and witness the flaring sky as the golden globe slips behind low-lying red hills.

After dinner we sit together on the large patio at a small table savoring the white wine and whispering winds of the Kalahari. Alex breaks the serene silence by saying, "Tomás, Lawrence of Arabia is my paternal grandfather and the Red Barron is my maternal grandfather. T.E. Lawrence had an affair with my German grandmother and here I am." She tells me she has his jaw. She also has his eyes and narrow face and walks like Lawrence probably walked, with a strident gait. This also may explain her reckless disregard for speed limits.

As Alex's family secret seeps into in my mind, a thick-bodied, thick-tongued young White man walks up to our table and strikes up a conversation. I invite Erick to join us. He refuses to sit down but stands like a stump in front of us talking in fractured Afrikaner English. Erick has been drinking rum and coke all evening with some other young Boers lounging at the pool bar. Alex proves very useful as an interpreter in this and other encounters with Boers in Namibia.

It seems that Erick wants to share his pain with sympathetic strangers. Erick is descended from Afrikaner farmers and is proud of his ancestry. He owns three farms and is struggling to survive economically in the Namibian drought. "Life will not improve for blacks in Namibia because they have no ambition," he says with conviction. "They have a different culture, a different way of living. Blacks are against modernization and progress. The Coloreds are better workers."

Erick is pessimistic about his future in Namibia. He fears he will lose his property (and his White privilege) due to President Sam Nujoma's steep increase in estate taxes, which he believes are part of a sinister plan to achieve with non-violence what President Mugabe is doing with violence in Zimbabwe: the redistribution of the land from the White owners to the Blacks.

Erick's diatribe is interrupted when a 4-wheel drive pulls up beside the pool and the young white guy behind the wheel yells out "Erick, let's get goin'." He shouts back, "I'm comin'" in a display of annoyance at the interruption. "I have to go." He says with some regret as he walks over to his ride, climbs in and takes off.

After a few glorious days wandering in the kaleidoscopic Kalahari we head north to Etosha National Wild Animal Park. The Red Baroness races on the rural white-gravel roads. I breathe a sigh of relief when we hit the paved four lane highway north to the capital Windhoek.

"Alex, slow down there's a roadblock ahead!"

She ignores me and doesn't apply her foot to the brakes until a police officer steps onto the road waving us to a stop on the roadside. Alex is pissed off. She jumps out of the car and argues with the cop who accuses her, rightfully, of speeding.

Reluctantly, I get out and follow her into a little shack with a desk where a few other officers are sitting around chewing the fat. At first they are amused by this white woman's pique. The officer's patience with her soon runs out. He orders her to shut up or be taken into custody. She turns red and fumes, but she does shut up. He hands her a ticket and tells her where to pay it. She takes the ticket and storms out of the office. I chase after her jumping in the car as she takes off like a fighter pilot on a mission.

That evening we arrive at a small town south of Etosha, check into a lodge and spend the night. The next day we buy a permit and cruise the park along with legions of tourists in vans, tour busses, trucks and cars. Despite the traffic we see a couple of lions, a few giraffe and other wildlife. Etosha is not like the Serengeti with its vast stretches of empty landscape and legions of animals living in a state of nature.

After a day in the wild animal park searching for wild life and dodging tourists we travel northwest to Kaokoland. We arrive in the lovely town of Kamanjab in the late afternoon. We stop at a quaint hotel on the edge of town. The lobby is empty and no one is behind the desk. I yell out for someone. A young white woman appears from an open door and says there are no vacancies and this is the only hotel in town. The place is fully booked because tomorrow is New Year's Eve. She refers us to a woman who rents cottages up the road. She also invites us to New Year's Eve dinner at the hotel.

Anxiously, we take off up a narrow gravel road until we reach a single story wood-framed house where we are warmly welcomed by a middle-aged white woman with a kind face. Helen is a widow who has lived in the area most of her life. She gives us a key and sends us up the road. When we reach the end of the road, we find a lovely stone cottage with a porch facing the setting sun.

By the time we clean up and settle into our idyllic digs, it's suppertime. We drive down the hillside on the earthen road past the small town and stop at a lodge. There we eat dinner and drink wine on the patio overlooking the guest rooms designed to look like an African village. The owner, a warm middle-aged Afrikaner woman, invites us to the lodge's New Year's Eve Party.

We slowly drive up the country road to our cottage on the edge of the wilderness. At sundown we bed down and dream in the screaming silence of Namibian night.

New Year's Eve we dine at the hotel with the other White guests. We meet the owner's brother, James, who lives with the Himba people. He joins us at our table for drinks after dinner. His story is fascinating and was featured in a European magazine article, "A White Man Goes Native." He fell in love with a Himba woman and the Himba culture. Then moved into the village, married his Himba lover and took on additional wives, per tradition. Although James wears typical western clothes at this New Year's Eve event, his Himba wives are conspicuously absent. I'm the only person of color at the dinner.

Alex and I resolve to visit the Himba people. On New Year's Day we set off early for the far northwest town of Kaoko, the capital of Kaokoland, home of the Himba tribe. On the way we pick up a hitchhiker standing on the side of the road. Henry is a school teacher fluent in English. Driven to distraction by Alex's driving, Henry entreats her to slow down. Surprisingly, she agrees.

As we slow down for a checkpoint before entering Kaoko, we see a fellow gesticulating between two uniformed men. When he sees us, he runs over and asks if we can give him a lift into town. We say yes and he gets in the back seat with Henry.

KK Muhuka works as a tour guide at the information center in Kaoko. He says he was being hassled by the authorities because he had forgotten his ID at home in the city. We drive into the bustling town in the late afternoon and KK directs us to a hotel. After dropping off Henry and KK, we check in and walk around the small town until nightfall when we eat and crash in tranquility.

In the morning, we pick up KK who has agreed to take us to the Himba village in Kaokoland. He has us buy sacks of flour and other provisions to give as gifts to the villagers. The village is a few miles north of the last paved road in northwest Namibia on the southern frontier of Angola. During the long drive KK gives us background on the Himba people.

"The Himba are a proud tribe of nomadic pastoralists who hold tenaciously to their rich cultural traditions. They are world renowned for their physical beauty, fine jewelry and traditional lifestyle. The Himba don't bathe or shower. Water is scarce in this desert region of the world. So they use smoke to clean their bodies every morning. Herbs and smoldering coals are placed in a container that produces smoke called *ombware*. It looks like a small pyramid of twigs. The Himba stand and sit in the sweet, musty smoke and their naked bodies are cleansed by it. Then they cover their bodies and hair with a mixture of butter fat and red ocher. The women wear their hair in long plaited braids. They also use herbal medicine and massage therapy to heal and cure disease and illness. For example they mix elephant dung with warm water to make a plaster that is applied to parts of the body afflicted by gout."

KK goes on to tell us, "The Himbas view sex as therapeutic. Having sex is like eating; you need it. You feel much better after sex. You are not stressed anymore. You can rest peacefully. However, having sex during the day is bad luck."

Then, KK delves into the supernatural side of Himba society. "The Holy Fire (*Okoruwo*) serves as the medium for communicating with the ancestral spirits." The Himba are an animist society based on the cult of ancestors. All fires in the village are lit by the Holy Fire. The *Onganga*, witchdoctor or shaman, performs all ceremonies and rituals associated with the Holy Fire.

"*Okoruwo* is used to heal and to celebrate and bless all major life events: birth, circumcision, marriage, death. The concept of death is very different from the Christian one. When a man physically dies, he is still present in the homestead. He still has duties to perform for two more generations to come. His name will still be called upon regularly. The Oruzo (patriclan) place each person in the position of having access to the infinite via his/her ancestors.

"The oldest living member of the patrilineage segment is designated as *Omuini Wokuruwo* (Keeper or possessor of the Holy Fire) and must preside at all functions pertaining to the *Okoruwo*. To each successive generation the *Okoruwo* will be known as the *Okoruwo* of the most recently deceased Keeper. His name will be invoked during the prayers to the deceased. The living Keeper, together with the deceased Keepers (whose names will be successively invoked as far back as they are known) form an unbroken chain stretching from the living generation all the way back to *Makuru* or God with whom the origin of humankind began. Blessings from *Makuru* and the deceased ancestors are available to the living members of the patrilineage."

When we arrive at the Himba village with its small rotund hide-covered huts, a tall regal bare-breasted woman who is traditionally attired in a leather skirt and wearing silver necklaces warmly greets us. KK introduces us to the head-woman and hands her the large sack of flour and other staples I bought in town. She invites us into her hut.

Inside we are introduced to the two smiling bare-breasted younger women who are sitting on the ground making jewelry. We squat on a mat spread on the ground as the women hand us various leather necklaces and bracelets, each with a conch inset. Smoke rises from the *ombware* purifying the air and adding a mysterious aura to the scene.

The head-woman is pounding herbs to create the ochre powder the women apply to their bodies. The women and children are very attractive and appear very content in their natural surroundings. The Himba have their front teeth removed. KK says that this is the custom, which KK rejected as a youth and explains why he has a full set of teeth. KK is a modern Himba who has abandoned the traditional life style to live and work in the city as a tour guide.

While the men are off working in the city and on the farms, the bare-breasted and barefoot women sit on the ground in the shade of a tree making jewelry and tending to their children.

After a pleasant exchange of smiles, giggles and conversation facilitated by KK with the head-woman and the ladies in the hut, Alex and I buy some jewelry. At dusk, after spending the day in the village we reluctantly say goodbye to these beautiful people and return to Kaoko for supper.

In the morning we head south to the mining town of Fransfontein where we enjoy a quiet lunch in a white-owned restaurant and bar. After lunch while filling the tank I buy some semi-precious stones from a local peddler passing by.

Alex drives southwest across the vast expanse of flat desert to the Skeleton Coast on the Atlantic where we finally arrive at Swakopmund. It's too late to return the car so we check into a hotel and crash.

The next morning after checking out of the hotel we discover a rear tire is flat. I have it repaired, then Alex drives us the final few blocks to return the car to the agency. The agent reminds me of Alex's moving violations. I pay the bill and fines and Alex walks out of the office and out of my life.

The next day I take the bus back to Windhoek where I meet a German gentleman with a Land Rover at the lodge. He is going to Capetown and offers me a ride south. A generous offer I cannot refuse.

Serengeti

Africa is billowy primrose clouds
on sky blue canvas
barefoot Masai boys wearing red plaid blankets
herding scrawny goats and cattle
over ruddy dry earth, purple green foothills—
our primal ancestral common ground

Thompson's gazelles graze sparse dry grass
giraffes browse on thorny treetops
loping in slow motion across the Serengeti plain—
ballet of pachyderms crossing in deep water single file
An elegant leopard languishes on naked limb of an ancient tree

African Princess

In a time capsule crossing Africa's Rift Valley
on Serengeti's vast plain a spirited young actress
Lady Emma and I are on the Ukimwi road together
on wildlife safari from Nairobi to Harare
our souls ignite in song, carefree and silly

Her playful laughter lulls me to sleep at sundown
I dream we are standing in the African bush—
she close behind me as I place my hands on hers

Together we thrill to thunder of the lion's roar
the flash of lightning
in dark cool Serengeti night—
until I am awakened by falling rain
and Emma's gleeful chatter at sunrise

Spice Island

Old spice swings with spice girls
on white sands of Zanzibar
seasoning the Indian Sea with
pepper, cinnamon, nutmeg, licorice
tamarin, coca, coffee, clove, aniseed...
and love for lady Emma

The grey gothic Anglican cathedral
stands on one side of a dreary stone wall
On the other is a sparkling white mosque
The old and the new separated by a wall
more solid than stone

Nyaminyami

Spirit god of the Zambezi River
runs through the heart of Africa
falling into Mosi Oa Tunya (Victoria Falls)
where rainbows span cascading
canyons of smoke that thunders
dagga rising like prayers
from the tonga pipe
of the Ndebele nation

Okavango Delta

The Rift Valley Everglade is replete
with water fowl, crocodiles, leaping frogs
and a myriad of marvelous insects
feeding in paradise

The regal fish eagle with sharp eyes & white skull soars
    high above
as sturdy Sericco poles our canoe through the rushes and reeds
under a canopy of rain clouds and sunshine until we reach
    bush camp

After we dig a trench for a latrine, pitch tents and light a fire
Sericco guides us through the wet bush where two bull
    elephants
loom close enough to inspire awe by their titanic presence

Tropical rain forever falling
while I wage a losing battle of slapping hands
against mosquito minions that pass through my netting
to sup in silence as I slumber
and dream of drowning

Uhuru Peak

On our fourth day of climbing Kili
we set off for the summit at midnight
with flaming hearts and numbing fatigue
we climb the steep gravel granite slope
pole! pole! slowly! slowly!

Thinning air causes catharsis at 5000 meters
I strain to lift and stretch leaden legs
to stand on a huge spinning stone
as searing pain grips my groin
I lose control of my gut

Promontories dance in purple haze
pole!   pole!   slowly! slowly!
each step an eternity
on the stairway to heaven

On Gilman's point sunrise signals its arrival
with silken banners spanning the horizon
then explodes in blinding sun

Postscript

It takes a lifetime of effort
and God's grace to reach the summit
Uhuru Peak
Freedom at 20,000 feet—

Jambo!

On the Silk Road

On the Road in Kerala

I'm riding the Kerala highway
with Father Thomas
the Indian Orthodox priest driving
in his white cassock and honking his horn
at rickshaws and sacred cows criss-crossing
the road as we pass over the Pampa River
that connects the people and land
with Christian, Muslim, Hebrew and Hindu
temples, mosques, synagogues and shrines
while listening to Elvis singing
"Don't you step on my blue suede shoes"

Seaside in Fort Kochi

As I sit on the waterfront
reading modern Malayalam verse
ravens swarm, swoop and swirl
in the tree tops
with choruses of caw...caw...caw
then light on fishing nets
billowing by the sea at sunset
as yesterdays' dreams vanish
in the ecstasy of fading day

Spice Scented India Night

While feasting on fish kebab curry and pineapple
lassi on a rooftop in Fort Kochi on Saturday night
a stream of smoke rises from the grill—
as a forest of florescent light from a Christian revival
casts an eerie glow over the weathered tile rooftops
shrouded in shadows below
a crescent moon cradled
in spice-scented Indian night

The Cave of the Heart

We climb the Chamundi Hills in Mysore
searching for the holy man
who dwells in a cave
on the summit and dispenses wisdom
to seekers of truth

Barefoot I bend over and enter
the deep cave of the heart
in search of the flame
that dispels the darkness that blinds

Sitting on a ledge in lotus position smiling
is Sannyasin Swamiji Jamanagiri
who in the glow of burning candles
and scent of sandalwood and incense
greets us with Sanskrit Vedic verse
and white lotus petals

He shares his Hindu vision of becoming
the lotus that rises from mud and water
blossoming in sun and air and moon and fire
the supreme spirit of Shiva
detached from the World
the Flesh and the Ego

Chanting in Sanskrit Vedic verse
he blesses me with white lotus petals
as we leave the cave of the heart with
love prayer and peace

Hari Raya

The rains come in the afternoon
turning the sultry streets of Jalan Sultan
into rivers scattering the shopkeepers
who huddle under their tarps and lean-tos
to shield their counterfeit watches
Gucci handbags, designer sports clothes
and tennis shoes from the weather

I sip my beer on the patio of the Swiss Inn
with pen in hand waiting for the wild one
who arrives at midnight to feed her feral hunger

"You have no inspiration only desperation"

She says as she struts away
to go shopping in the night market
leaving me on the patio with pen in hand
hope sinking with the setting sun

Suddenly the rain stops
and the streets come alive
the fasting and prayers end
and the feasting begin again

A Salaam Alaikum

Koh Phan Ngan

I leave the rowdy bars of Koh Samui
for the quiet of Koh Phan Ngan
where there is no place to sleep
on the winter solstice

The sign says
"All full, free beds, showers next to the police station"

Jim, the crusty good-humored Englishman
and his smiling young wife, Choi
take me in for a few baht a night
as strains of Satchmo's coronet
drift across the harbor

Thai sun bakes white sand
by day and barking dogs
patrol the beach at dusk

A big mangy dog
with dangling balls
is boss of the beach

He sniffs and lifts his hind leg
anywhere without challenge
Smaller dogs fearing his jaws
scurry through the palms

As the yellow lantern slowly sinks
into shimmering pea green sea
I swing and sway on my hammock
on the porch of my bungalow
filing my memories away
with the passing of another day

Buddha

Buddha sits under a shady tree
on a breezy Saturday
on the bank of the meandering Mekong
He measures the passage of sunlight
from the summit of a timeless pine
to the settled earth—
scoring the rhythm of rustling wind
in lofty green hills of Laos
melding at sundown
with melodies of night

Dalat

It is raining in the hills
above the karaoke bars of Saigon

Buddha sits serenely smiling
on a billowy cloud

in his golden temple
in the silver mist of summer

Hoi An

Red, yellow and lavender lanterns
lie the flooding river banks
as dark water spreads in silence
through the sleeping streets of Hoi An
as water falls
from a gloaming sky

Thuy

Destiny introduces me to
a slender reed
balancing a lotus blossom
wearing an áo dái

We meet in the Imperial garden
of the Citadel
on a cool wet afternoon

You walk softly among the ruins
of the Tet Offensive
on vast graveyard grass
in reverence for the fallen
from both sides

You live in Ho Chi Minh City
and work in the Guitar Bar
Your black hair, alabaster skin
and sparkling eyes
are as stunning
as colorful pavilions and temples
royal palaces and galleries
surrounded by stonewalls

The camera's eye catches you
as you place your right forefinger
between left forefinger and thumb

Smiling you say
"I'll see you in Saigon"
Hope swells then fades
as Thuy rejoins the spirits of Tet
on holiday in Huê

Angkor Wat

The city which is a temple
rises from the ruins of Nixon's secret war
and the Khmer Rouge killing fields

Majestic replica of the cosmos
mystical temples of stone
rows of filigreed towers
rise from the Perfume river

Causeways flanked by serpent balustrades
lead to cross-shaped terraces
where a steep stairway lined with lions
leads to the shrine of Vishnu
who greets strangers with eight arms

Asparas, bare-breasted celestial dancers
emerge from temple walls and stairways
A Khmer poet once wrote
"They were never carved by the hands of men!
They were created by the gods—
living, lovely, breathing women"

Torches flame on stone altars in dark corridors
where squatting saffron robed priests chant
in galleries as girls in diaphanous gowns
dance up and down stone stairways
in clouds of incense rising like prayers
from lotus blossoms floating in clay pots

The barren royal library
now bereft of literary treasures
leads to the gallery of 1000 Buddhas
and the Hall of Echoes
where the Bagavata Pourana says

"The Ocean of Milk is churned by the gods
and demons to generate Amrta, the elixir
of life and immortality"

Risking the wrath of King Saryavarman
I water in a dark corner of the temple
his remains with mine

Vision Quest

San Ignacio

It's the week before Christmas 1982, and Ricardo, my sturdy middle-aged Chicano *amigo* and I are traveling south in my black Rabbit convertible, Proud Mary. We fly past gray brown hills and small mountains of piled stones with varieties of cactus blossoming in Baja's hot sun. This is California before white America took over Alta California and made it into endless freeways, *barrios*, Hollywood Hills, track housing and Disneyland. We're not sure of our destination but we know we're headed in the right direction, south into Baja, California and away from San Diego, USA.

In the late morning of our second day on the road we drive through the narrow archway of the walled entrance to San Ignacio, the old mission town in the heart of God's creation in the middle of Baja. The imposing Spanish colonial church of San Ignacio stands like a fortress on the west side of the plaza. The church was designed by Spanish Jesuits and built on the backs of the local Indians whose bones are interred in the thick stone walls and whose spirits dwell in the vaulted ceiling and wooden beams.

Once inside the church, a tall, life-size statue of the black Peruvian saint, San Martin De Porres, wearing his white habit and black tunic, greets us. His extended black hand holds a loaf of bread offered to pilgrims to his shrine. I'm very fond of San Martin De Porres. He was the first and only black saint I discovered in my youth and his statue overlooked the desk in my cluttered bedroom in the back of the house.

At nightfall, the village children process around the church with hand-held candles illuminating their angelic faces. While they process around the church they recite La Posada liturgy of rejection by mankind of the Virgin Mother, Theotokos, and her faithful husband, Joseph, seeking lodging to give birth to the Savior. According to St. John's gospel, "And the Word was made flesh, and dwelt among us. He was in the world, and world was made by him, and the world knew him not. He came unto his own, and his own received him not."

Fr. Primo, the old Italian mission priest, leads his brown cherubs through the open church doors into the glowing sanctuary where the *crèche* waits the light of the world. The church has worn-smooth wooden pews, sturdy, roughly hewn rafters, stone floor, fortress-like walls and a rococo *reredos*.

Inspired we leave the church before nightfall and drive past the plaza to La Posada Motel on the eastern edge of town. There we meet gregarious Pedro, the potbellied owner of the motel, who tells us about his father who killed himself with kerosene and a match after Pedro insisted he pay rent to live on the property his father had given him. Then Pedro offers to take us in the morning to the newly discovered Indian cave paintings (petroglyphs) that are thousands of years old. Bewildered and exhausted we accept his offer and retreat into our rustic room with its twin beds and crash.

Before sunrise we ride into the desert in the back of Pedro's pickup huddling under blankets in the frosty early morning air as our lean smiling Indian guide, Juaquin, navigates across the barren brown wilderness to our destination, relics of ancestral earthen spirits. We pass a variety of cactus: cirios, cholla and cardones, standing with arms uplifted like tall green shamans welcoming us to the secrets of the land.

After a long ride we ascend a gentle rise and stop before a simply constructed single-story wooden shed. A *caballero* wearing a straw-sombrero, leather chaps, boots and spurs, rides into the yard on a hazel-hued horse. He dismounts, removes the saddle and carries it into the open shed. Meanwhile, his children laugh and play as his wife stands in the humble adobe doorway watching us.

We leave the pickup at the *hacienda* and follow Juaquin through the stands of cacti, up the rugged hillside to a huge cave hidden in the hillside. I stand in the mouth of the cave staring at its massive gray walls covered with stylistic images of mesquite, wild deer, buffalo, dogs, cats, and spirit dancers.

The dark image of a shaman looms high on the far cave wall facing the opening. One side of the shaman's body is black and the other rouge. He stands in the sacred circle of fire with arms and hands outstretched entreating the benevolent spirits to shield them from any evil forces lurking in the night. Shamans commune with desert spirits dwelling in prickly cacti, crawling creatures, pulverized rock and bones.

The next morning after *huevos y frijoles* we stroll out of town onto a barren landscape of sand, stone and cactus. There we encounter the low rock wall of the village cemetery. We step over the wall where wooden crosses rise before sandstone sepulchers festooned with brightly colored flowers. We stand in the sacred shaman circle of small stones and bleached bones surrounded by pristine purple mountains and cactus groves communing with abiding indigenous spirits.

We return to town in the silence of nightfall and cross the empty town plaza to the corner store where we buy beer and other provisions for third night of Christmas in this tranquil village. Our lively conversation with the local merchant and a small group of good-natured young men congregating in the store is interrupted by shouting voices from outside in the darkness. We rush out to join a few locals standing in front of the darkened church, with eyes staring and fingers pointing into the starry night.

We gaze above at the tubular-shaped object enshrouded in hazy phosphorescence hovering in the western sky then moving slowly in a southerly direction behind the dark specter of the church tower. We walk along the plaza gazing up at the enigma and wondering aloud "What is it?" "I think it's a dirigible," Ric replies. I'm skeptical. What's a blimp doing here at this hour? When we reach the southwestern edge of the plaza weary of watching the strange object we turn and start walking to La Posada. The voice of the town drunk lurking in the dark beckons us. "*Mira!*" he shouts, pointing to the sky, "*Mira!*" We turn and see the mysterious object now emitting a beacon of white light into the northern sky. Suddenly, it disappears. I run up the stone stairway climbing the church tower and peer at the sky. All I see in the star studded night is a purple haze where the object once hovered. Amazed by this cosmic vision on this quiet night in this humble *pueblo* in the middle of Baja we trudge back on the rutted dirt road to the La Posada cantina for a meal.

We enter the small brightly lit dining room and sit at a small table. We order beers and *arroz y pollo*. At a small table by the window sits Jim, an old-timer from Wyoming, who wears his long white hair in a ponytail. Jim's daughter is an artist researching pre-historic indigenous cave paintings in the hills outside of San Ignacio. She is camping out in the caves and he is staying at the motel. A stocky, moon-faced bearded man and an attractive brunette with lovely long legs occupy a table beside the bar. They are deep in hushed conversation.

Over dinner Ric and I discuss the celestial vision we witnessed: the white light emanating from the tubular shaped object hovering in heavenly phosphorescent light, then disappearing in starry night sky leaving a purple haze. The moon-faced man now joins in our conversation. He is curious about our sighting. We get into a heated discussion of UFOs. We finally introduce ourselves. The bearded guy is Carlos Castañeda and his lady friend is Diana. I ask him if he is the author Carlos Castañeda who writes the books on Yaqui wisdom. He replies, "*Si*, that's me." I am stunned. Carlos and Diana have just spent two nights sleeping in the Indian caves. Carlos is seeking inspiration for his next book. I ask Carlos about Don Juan and Yaqui wisdom. "Have you met other sorcerers in Yaqui land and what have they taught you?" The subject shifts from the extraterrestrial to the mystical.

After dinner the night air is buzzing with cosmic energy. As Ric and I turn to head to our room we hear a voice behind us "How about a couple of joints?" It's Carlos. Surprised Ric says, "Sorry, no rolling papers, only a pipe. If you want some smoke you can join us in our room." Carlos and Diana follow us into our motel room. Ric sits at the end of his bed facing Carlos who sits on a small chair next to a small desk. Diane sits to Ric's left with her back to the door and stretches her long legs. I sit on my bed fixing a pipe. After sharing cholla juice and sensimilla, the next fantasy phase begins.

Stoned Carlos speaks in staccato and has a nervous twitch. Ric, the gregarious Chicano psychotherapist, blurts out. "I didn't think you actually existed."

Carlos leans forward in his chair, his face raised close to Ric's and whispers, "Do you believe I exist now?"

Ric recoils from the blow and laughs nervously. "If you say you are Carlos Castañeda, who am I to doubt you?" Then he begins peppering Carlos with questions about the ways of the Yaqui, since Ric is a descendent of the Yaqui on his mother's side of the family and considers himself an expert on the subject. They get into a deep dialogue and psychic duel on the Yaqui way of wisdom with Carlos firing rapid responses to Ric's questions and comments.

After Carlos gets hyped up on sensemilla and a few shots of cholla juice, he asks us if we are reporters and if we are secretly taping him.

"Everything's cool. We are poets, not reporters. Be cool," I implore. After witnessing intense Yaqui sorcery between Ric and Carlos, Diana and I go from stoned to exhausted. Diana smiles and says, "Good night." Carlos jumps up without saying a word and hurries after Diana into the night. I collapse on my narrow bed hallucinating cacti in bright yellows, greens and reds.

Later, as Ric and I soar into comatose cosmic consciousness we hear a knock at the door. Ric gets up and opens the door. There silhouetted by moonlight in the frame of the doorway stands Carlos Castañeda. Ric faces Carlos, his back to me. Trancelike, they exchange Yaqui karma until the spell is broken when Carlos blurts out, "Goodnight." Ric closes the door and I fall into deep Yaqui dream time.

On Christmas Day, we rise early to say goodbye to the spirits dwelling in the caves and on holy cemetery ground. After *tortillas, huevos y frijoles* we pack up and drive past the village square waving goodbye. We pass through the narrow stone archway on our way out of the village. We drive northwest to Guerrero Negro then due north to cross *la frontera* serenaded by Miles' *Sketches of Spain* as the sun spreads golden over the southern desert.

Mexican Enigma

It is spring of 2005 and after a month on the road in Mexico I am amazed at how this nation of over 100 million people can cohere in such a state of economic inequality and social conflict.

My journey begins in Tijuana where I fly early in the morning to Leon, high in the hills of central Mexico. From there I share a ride with a lovely new friend to the provincial colonial city of Guanajuato. My room in la Casa Bertha overlooks the adobe tile-roofed city built on steep slopes with narrow streets twisting around hillsides then disappearing into tunnels.

The next morning I walk down the hill to *la basilica* on Plaza de la Paz where I run into a brass band leading twelve men bearing on their shoulders a plaster statue of the Virgin of Guanajuato followed by an endless procession of pilgrims winding through the city's teeming cobblestone streets. In May, the month of Mary, there are three processions a week commemorating Our Lady on the streets of Guanajuato. All led by a loud brass band and a legion of spirited drummers.

Alternating with the public devotions to the Blessed Virgin Mary are the protest marches through the heart of the city led by Marxist *sindicatos*, trade unions and *anarchistas* waving red banners and clamoring for social and economic justice. These social activists gather in front of El Jardín de la Union (The Garden Plaza) where militants deliver fiery speeches attacking the status quo. One speaker asks the crowd to reach into their pockets and pull out some pesos. When the crowd stands with pesos in raised hands he directs us to give them to the person standing next to us. A practical lesson in selfless socialism I had never witnessed before and may never see again.

As I walk away from the red banners and speeches I pass the outdoor restaurants and cafés shaded by trees lining El Jardín de la Union. There sit the wealthy tourists and rich fair-skinned Mexicans eating their gourmet meals on white table cloths impervious to the revolutionary voices seeking to redistribute their wealth.

My next stop is the highly-hyped tourist town of San Miguel de Allende an hour's drive from Guanajato. I roll into town and settle into the comfy hotel recommended by my artist friend Conchita Amata. *La proprietaria* reminds me how *muy rico* and expensive the city is and how lucky I am to have gotten such a good price for my room with a view of the terra cotta tile-roofed colonial city.

For a few days and nights I wander through the cobblestone streets and plazas visiting the art galleries and bars. I meet and converse with several resident expatriates and tourists. San Miguel has become a quaint, colonial Mexican theme park designed to serve the needs of the over 10,000 retired gringos living here.

After luxuriating in the natural mineral hot springs at Balnearios on the outskirts of town, I hitch a ride to Querétaro where the Mexican war of independence was born. I walk to the heart of the historical old town Jardín Zenea where I visit a museum featuring art protesting the United States war in Iraq. After the anti-war art show, I eat lunch at an outdoor café facing the plaza. The next day I take off for the south on a night bus that features a Hollywood action movie starring Arnold Schwarzenegger.

After a long bus ride I finally arrive in the intriguing southwestern state capital of Oaxaca. Oaxaca is famous for its indigenous handicrafts, silk scarves and mole. I soon discover it's also known for its militant Marxist-Leninist *sindicatos*. When I take my morning walk to *el zócalo* (central plaza) I see a sea of blue tarps and tents strung across the streets and sidewalks. The 75,000 strong state teacher's union is on strike and teachers instead of teaching in the classroom are occupying the center of the city.

The strikers have closed all of the public schools in the state of Oaxaca for a month. They gather in small groups under their tarps and plan strategies to obtain higher salaries and better working conditions. They march through the city waving red banners and carrying large posters of Marx, Lenin, Engels and even Joseph Stalin. How ironic that this devout Roman Catholic country has some of the most militant and radical unions and political parties in the Americas.

I am impressed by the organizational skill and cohesion the strikers display. Everyone is well-behaved and takes their task of raising consciousness seriously. The city manages without any police/protestor confrontations or disturbances. There is no vehicular traffic in the heart of the city until the teachers disband after a week of peaceful street protests.

I marvel at the richly carved baroque façade of La Basílica de la Soledad and wonder how many Indians and Blacks lost their lives building these elaborate golden temples and basilicas to the Virgin Mary. Mexico's patron is Our Lady of Guadalupe and May is her month. However, after sundown from my hotel window, I see scantily clad sexy ladies soliciting in the shadows on the street below.

After a couple days of wandering the occupied tent city of Oaxaca, I travel by bus two hours to the birthplace of Benito Juarez, the small town of Guelatao. Benito Júarez was the great reforming leader of 19th century Mexico and a full-blooded Zapotec. He served two terms as Oaxaca State Governor before being elected Mexico's President in 1861. He had been in office only a few months when France, supported by the Catholic Church, invaded Mexico and forced him into exile. In 1867, Júarez ousted the French and their puppet emperor, Maximilian. Benito Júarez died in 1872, a year after being elected to his fourth presidential term. Countless statues, streets, schools and plazas preserve his name and memory, and his sage maxim: '*El respeto al derecho ajeno es la paz*' (Respect for the rights of others is peace). I pay my respects to one of the greatest political leaders in the history of the Americas.

It's late afternoon and the cooling rains of Springtime have come and gone. Dark clouds have scattered behind pine covered hills surrounding the colonial city of San Cristóbal de las Casas. The sky is luminous blue as the sun smiles on the cobblestone streets and tiled roofs of this tranquil small town. Here in Meso-America paradox prevails. This is where high-tech converges with pre-Vatican II Roman Catholicism and the pre-Columbian world of the Olmecs (some say Mexico's mother culture), Tzotzils and Tzeltals, ancestors of the Mayans.

This is where on January 1, 1994, the Zapatista guerillas emerged from the hills and forests to occupy San Cristóbal and other towns in Chiapas. The Zapatistas are the armed vanguard in the fight on behalf of the underrepresented and oppressed indigenous people that constitute half the population of Chiapas. There is still strong support for the Zapatistas in the indigenous villages and towns surrounding San Cristóbal, especially in San Juan Chamula and Zincantan.

The Tzotzil village of Chamula focuses on the mystical church of St. John the Baptist. Here in the sanctuary on the floor strewn with pine needles before the high altar stands plaster statues of the saints. Throngs of locals gather in groups to perform esoteric acts of healing and animal sacrifice while chanting in an ethereal language as clouds of incense rise above statues. Hundreds of flaming candles are stuck to the floor by men wearing white woolen ponchos and white head scarves. These are the people who expelled thousands of fellow Chamulas from their villages for converting to Protestantism brought by U.S. evangelical missionaries.

Chiapas is a rare place where one can witness the convergence and clash of cultures while at the same time achieve spiritual insight and inspiration from the indigenous people. There is a thriving Buddhist prayer and meditation center in San Cristóbal where dharma classes and meditation sessions are led by the Venerable Gueshe Kelsang Gyato. While trekking to remote villages in the hills and exploring Mayan ruins in Palenque, one finds peace of mind, where all spiritual paths converge.

Mexico's Forgotten Negros

One day while wandering around El Zócalo I meet Juan, a fair-complexioned *mestizo* owner of a travel agency in San Cristóbal de Las Casas, Chiapas. I ask him about the former slave chapel of San Nicolas behind the Cathedral just across from his office on El Zócalo. Juan's response, "Tomás, there have never been any black slaves in San Cristóbal." I open my journal and read to him the words I copied from the historical notice posted at the entrance to the chapel.

> *Alrededor de 1615, el obisbo Juan de Zapata y Sandoval fundó´ la ermita de San Nicolas de los Morenos para la confraria negra de Nuestra Señora de la Encarnación, la cual, en contra de lo acostumbrado en el caso de iglesias para negros y mulatos, se hizo en el centro de la ciudad. Fue el primer templo formal de la ciudad.*

> *(Around 1615 the bishop Juan de Zapata y Sandoval founded the hermitage of San Nicolas of the dark ones for the confraternity of Our Lady of the Incarnation, which, contrary to custom in the case of churches for Negroes and mulattos, he placed in the center of the city. It was the first formal temple of the city.)*

Juan, an intelligent man who once lived in La Jolla, California, still insists that, "There never were any *Negros* in San Cristóbal." Juan's disturbing response is, regrettably, all too typical and misinformed. Africans were brought to Mexico 500 years ago as slaves to replace the indigenous population decimated by Spanish conquest and disease. Blacks have been in Mexico ever since, though their presence has been virtually ignored and underestimated until recent times.

"The Black population is not well known," says Sagrario Cruz, anthropology and history professor at the University of Veracruz, which offers the multidisciplinary program, *Africa en Mexico*. She has documented distinct populations of slaves, maroons, black Seminoles and U.S. Blacks, both free people and runaway slaves, who settled in the country before and after Mexico abolished slavery. Free Blacks have lived in Mexico since as early as 1609. The two generals who led Mexico's war of independence from Spain, José María Morelos and Vicente Guerrero, after Father Hidalgo was executed by the Spanish in 1811, were of African ancestry. "El Negro Guerrero" was the second president of Mexico and he abolished slavery in 1829.

Henry Louis Gates, Jr.'s book and television documentary, *Black in Latin America* along with two other documentaries from Mexico, *The Forgotten Roots* and *African Blood*, recount the strong African heritage that has endured centuries of neglect in Mexico. These works show most *Afromestizos* or Afro-Mexicans are concentrated in the state of Veracruz on the Gulf Coast and in the states of Guerrero and Oaxaca on la Costa Chica (Little Coast) region on the Pacific Coast. La Costa Chica is a 200-mile long coastal region that begins just south of Acapulco and ends in Puerto Angel, Oaxaca. Together with Chiapas, they make up the three poorest states in Mexico.

In Veracruz, on the Caribbean coast, African culture and heritage persist most strongly in dance, music and song. They even have a museum celebrating Mexico's African heritage. However, on the Pacific Coast, African culture and tradition have been largely forgotten and lost to posterity.

After Chiapas my next stop in my search for the African diasporas is La Costa Chica on the Pacific coast of the state of Oaxaca. In the city of Pinotepa I call the Rev. Father Glyn Jemmott. Padre Glyn is the Roman Catholic priest from Trinidad, West Indies, who since 1984 has served as vicar to several Afro-Mexican towns on la Costa Chica. I met Padre Glyn the year before at a symposium on black Mexico at the University of California San Diego. He invited me to visit him in La Costa Chica and I gladly accepted.

Early the next morning, I travel by taxi to meet Padre Glyn in the nearby village of El Ciruelo. As the taxi cruises into town I can see from the complexion of the people that I have arrived in black Mexico. The driver drops me off at village church where Padre Glyn gives me a warm welcome. Padre tells me dozens of Afro-Mexican communities lie in La Costa Chica, barely subsisting from farming and fishing. Over the next few days Padre Glyn drives me to several of these communities where I meet many of his parishioners. In the lakeside town of El Corralero I attend mass and listen to the Padre's homily on the pride of Afro-Mexicans. Padre Glyn estimates the Afro-Mexican population of Mexico at three to ten percent depending on who is counting and who acknowledges African ancestry. The federal government does not count Blacks as a separate minority. Instead Afro-Mexicans are largely ignored by government services, marginalized by racist attitudes and relegated to lives of poverty and illiteracy, on the fringes of Mexican society.

According to Professor Cruz, "The problem of the loss of cultural identity, along with that of racial discrimination, is that even some black people will deny their own racial heritage." The spurious practice of *mejorando la raza,* literally "bettering the race," by marrying someone lighter-skinned than oneself, is alive and well in Mexico.

For example, when I meet Pedro, a handsome young Afro-Mexican man in the lobby of one of Pinotepa's finer hotels, he initially denies his African heritage. After I explain to Pedro that I am an African American researching the African diaspora in Mexico, he grudgingly admits to having a black grandparent.

As I bid *adios* to black Mexico, Presidente Vincente Fox apologizes to black Americans for saying "Undocumented Mexicans living in the USA don't take jobs away from Americans, they do jobs that not even black Americans will do." However, he refuses to remove from circulation the racist, stereotyping "Sambo stamp" of *Memin Pinguin* and of course, he refuses to apologize to Mexico's forgotten *Negros.*

After a day of riding the bus and enjoying the scenery on the route north, I finally arrive at the granddaddy of Mexican coastal resorts once called "The Pearl of the Pacific." The crescent city of Acapulco rises beside La Bahía de Acapulco. The curving coastline with its sandy white beaches and palm trees is lined by rows of luxury tourist hotels, restaurants and nightclubs. Here, one can easily idle away the sunny days and nights in a reverie of overindulgence. I avoid tourist row along *El Malecón* and check into the colonial style Hotel Mission in Old Acapulco, only a few blocks from El Zócalo and the harbor.

While crossing El Zócalo I am waylaid by a short stocky black Mexican with a wild Afro. Jose offers to show me the central market. I tag along while he leads the way across crowded streets and sidewalks until we arrive at the bustling open market place. I look at lots of jewelry and precious stones, then pay him some pesos and excuse myself.

The next day I ride a bus the full length of hotel row along the harbor where the jet setters hang out. The economy is tourist-dependent with a plethora of shops selling art and handicrafts from the region. One day while sitting at a café on the edge of El Zócalo sipping a cup of herbal tea I introduce myself to a lovely *mulata* maiden named María. I invite her to lunch. She joins me and tells me about her life in the state of Guerrero. I discuss with her my research on the African diaspora in Mexico and my recent visit to la Costa Chica. Maria tells me, "Tomás, there are many *Negros* in the state of Guerrero and the governor is a *mulato.* The state of Guerrero is named after Vicente Ramón Guerrero, the Afro-Mexican general who is the George Washington of Mexico." After lunch we visit some art galleries in the old colonial city and we say goodbye, promising to meet again for an evening of salsa at Nina's nightclub and disco.

Before leaving Acapulco, I spend a day climbing and roaming around Isla Roqueta. Except for the throngs of Mexican tourists packing the beach next to the landing and the military outpost on the summit I find the island largely deserted. I trudge along on the cliffs high above the striking coastline and sparkling sea. I descend to a quiet harbor where I disrobe and dive into the soft blue water without seeing a soul until I return to the landing for the boat ride back to the tourist town.

After leaving Acapulco, I arrive in el Distrito Federal with its gargantuan urban sprawl and smog, its chronic traffic jams and taxi crime. The metro offers a clean, inexpensive and efficient subway system that provides a welcome reprieve from frenetic surface travel. I take the metro to visit the city's cultural and artistic Mecca near El Zocaló and Alameda Central Park. Mexico City is blessed with a gold mine of museums, galleries and churches. I feed my soul on the power and passion of Diego Rivera, Orozco and Frieda Kahlo.

Mexico City's popular mayor, Andrés Manuel López Obrador, of the PRD, is the leading contender in the following year's presidential election. The poor and progressives see López Obrador as the leading voice for social and economic justice in Mexico.

For Mexico's economic elite, López Obrador is seen as a threat to their institutional power and privilege. For this reason the rich ruling class resents and fears him. The government of Presidente Fox was forced to end its criminal investigation of López Obrador when over a million Mexicans marched in the streets protesting what they perceived as an illicit attempt to disqualify Obrador from running in Mexico's 2006 presidential election, an election which he lost.

I fly from Mexico City to Baja where I spend several days on La Bahía de La Paz sitting on the palm-lined seafront promenade sipping a daiquiri and feasting on *ceviche* as streaks of setting sun sink into la bahía. Then, I spend a day in the Pacific coastal town of Todos Santos. I stroll the narrow streets of this quaint small town basking in art galleries and mellow gatherings in sidewalk cafés. I end my day lounging and lunching in the celebrated Hotel California.

From La Paz I travel north by bus past several military checkpoints where soldiers search passenger luggage for contraband. After a bus ride lasting several hours through spectacular landscapes of desert promontories, blue sea and white sand, I arrive in Mulegé, a delightful town on the Sea of Cortez. I soon discover there is neither a bank nor an ATM in this quiet little tourist town but I have enough cash to buy a colorful rug and a sombrero. The sun is oven-hot at midday so the entire town goes on siesta from late morning until late afternoon. For relief from the heat I swim in the sea. The cool water is turquoise blue and transparent. I swim in a fantasy of flashing colorful fish and slippery rocks and coral. At dusk I have my first and last ice massage given by the lovely princess of pain who owns a spa overlooking the village and the sea.

Leaving the Sea of Cortez, I traverse the Transpeninsular Highway through a landscape of mesquite, ocotillo, cholla, chaparral, sage and towering cordon cacti to Guerrero Negro on the Pacific Coast. From there it's only a matter of hours before I arrive in Tijuana and cross *la frontera* into San Diego.

Muy amable Mexico maintains cultural cohesion because of its heritage of strong family values derived from the indigenous heritage and the Roman Catholic Church. With its emphasis on family and tradition, Mexico has thus far been able to survive the vicissitudes of political corruption and economic exploitation. However, the Recession and Mexico's belated entry into America's war on drugs has compounded Mexico's social/economic problems and paint a bleak picture for its future.

Diamonds in the Dark

The pale half moon
with her ghostly silver halo
hangs in star-studded sky
smiling at the quiet casas
sitting silent on the hill
as the urban river flows
through the canyons
winding its way south
to the border
where on the other side
lights flicker
like diamonds in the dark

71

Tapatío

Chiming church bells in Colonia Americana
rouse me from tequila dreams
of white swans soaring over Lake Chapala
I dress, eat my oatmeal and banana
and begin another day
in Guadalajara with its baroque basilicas
plaster saints and bustling plazas
Where sensuous *señoritas* wearing stilettoes
bursting blouses and designer jeans stroll
on cracked sidewalks and cobblestone streets
Their dark eyes sparkling
on Calle La Paz and Boulevard Chapultepec
where young men in dreadlocks and Indian women
display bracelets, trinkets and charms
as corpulent kids munch on chicharrones
and sup sodas while I wander
on my way to la Feria Internacional del Libro
where we gather together to worship
at the altar of the written word made flesh

On the Inca Trail

On the Inca Trail

My friend from San Diego, Solar Man, meets me at my hotel and after I check in, we walk down Calle Quilca in the Chincha district of colonial Lima at sundown where clusters of mostly men and boys stand on the cobblestone street debating and listening to exhortations from passionate speakers on various subjects from the cost of coca to the despised *Presidente* Toledo. I purchase a volume of César Vallejo's poetry from a funky bookstore on Calle Quilca. Then Solar Man and I stop at La Noche café/bar and down pisco sours as the locals pass by in the dark.

After Solar Man disappears, I wander farther down the darkened walkway to see murals flaming on dreary brick walls made by passionate artists who gather at El Averno gallery to plot and to paint anarchistic art in the side streets and alleys of Lima. At the end of Calle Quilca I turn the corner onto the teeming Plaza San Martín where the bronze liberator sits elegantly astride his bronze horse. I visit the baroque churches with their gaudy statues and sodalities to the Blessed Virgin Mary and her suffering son skewered to the cross, bathed in blood and wearing a red Inca skirt.

Finally I arrive at the tomb of my favorite saint, St. Martin de Porres. As the SQP Network website http://saints.sqpn.com/saint-martin-de-porres/ describes:

"[Martin was] the illegitimate son of a Spanish nobleman, Juan, and a young freed black slave, Anna Velasquez. Martin grew up in poverty. He spent part of his youth with a surgeon-barber from whom he learned some medicine and care of the sick. At age 11 Martin became a servant in the Holy Rosary Dominican Priory in Lima, Peru. Where he begged more than $2,000 a week from the rich to support the poor and sick of Lima. Placed in charge of the Dominican's infirmary he was known for his tender care of the sick and for his spectacular cures. His superiors dropped the stipulation that "No black person may be received to the holy habit or profession of our

order" and Martin took vows as a Dominican brother in 1603.
Martin established an orphanage and children's hospital for
the poor children of the slums. He set up a shelter for the stray
cats and dogs and nursed them back to health. He lived in
self-imposed austerity, never ate meat, fasted continuously,
and spent much time in prayer and meditation with a great
devotion to the Holy Eucharist. He was venerated from the
day of his death. Many miraculous cures, including raising the
dead, are attributed to Brother Martin, the first canonized
black saint from the Americas."

After I light a candle and kneel before St. Martin's small grey skull displayed on a side altar, I rise and walk out into a bustling colonial city.

I travel 100 miles south of the nation's capital, Lima, to the Afro-Peruvian region called Chincha, home to the country's largest concentration of black Peruvians. Within Chincha, the village of El Carmen in Chincha is considered the Afro-Peruvian cultural center where festivals are celebrated with Afro-Peruvian music, dance, food and drink. After an endless drive through the countryside in a local taxi we see lights and hear music as we pass a sign that reads, "El Carmen: Peru's Capital of Black folklore." The town square is jammed with people ready to kick off the festivities in celebration of both Christmas and the Virgin of El Carmen. The taxi driver tells me that over the Christmas holiday, the townspeople put on a four-day celebration culminating in the Day of the Virgin of El Carmen, an all-night, all-day gala that pays tribute to the town's patron saint.

Brightly dressed folks flow from the church yard following Christmas Eve Midnight Mass while others gather in the park eating *anticuchos* (beef hearts roasted on a stick) with fries dipped in spicy salsa and drinking a potent home brew called *tutuma*, made from pisco (grape liquor). Meanwhile children sing and dance to the Afro-Peruvian beat blasting from the musicians jammin' on the street and I am struck by the several shades of black.

In 1532, when Spanish conquistadors arrived to seize Peru from the Incan people, African slaves accompanied them. The country's Black population began to increase markedly several decades later, when Africans from the Bantu regions were captured by Spaniards and brought to Peru as slaves. By 1570, census takers counted more Blacks than Spaniards in coastal Peru. Some historians believe that even as late as the mid-1700s half of the population of Lima was of African origin. After slavery was abolished in 1854, Incan and Aymaran peoples from the mountain regions flooded the cities in search of work. They mixed with the local Black population and became part of the workforce and the official census count.

The taxi drops me off at the single-story white stucco *casita* of Amador Ballumbrosio, one of Peru's leading songwriters, vocalists and a master violinist who embodies the Afro-Peruvian cultural tradition. I knock on the rustic wooden door and a matronly black woman opens it. I introduce myself and explain my mission to her. She smiles and invites me inside. She is Amador's wife. She excuses herself and wheels in a dark-skinned old man with gray hair. Don Amador sits in his wheelchair holding his violin and reminiscing about the old days. Because of Amador and others like him Afro-Peruvian traditions and culture have survived and prospered in Peru. He and his lovely wife have lived in El Carmen all their lives. Even though he is unsure about the path of his ancestors from Africa to Peru, the music and dance that his father taught him clearly recalls the sounds and rhythms of West Africa.

On a sunny Sunday morning, I sit on the empty patio sipping *mate de coca*, pen in hand eating bread and blackberry jam, meditating on white vapor hovering over majestic Mt. Misty.

After breakfast I walk down a cobblestone street to El Convento de Santa Catalina, a former nunnery. Here, divided by caste, the lowly Indians waited hand and foot on the privileged Spanish and middle-class Mestiza nuns. The nuns were finally forced by a papal bull to live like a religious community instead of a walled wealthy female town in the heart of the city.

I visit the kneeling sculpted figure and frozen face of Juanita whose young life was sacrificed on a mountain top by Incan priests in propitiation for the sins of her people and to please Pacha Mama (Mother Earth) and Hanang Pacha (Father Heaven).

In late afternoon I dine at a quaint local restaurant and while sipping on pisco sours I engage *una linda señorita* in a conversation about local social mores. She smiles and says:

Mira Tomasito, aquí las chicas somos un poco lentas.
Esperamos que primero ustedes den el primero paso...
Y luego uyuyuy! Ten cuidado!
Por algo somos Latinas!

(Look it Tomasito, here the girls are a little slow.
We wait until you make the first pass...
And then uyuyuy! Take care!
For after all we are Latinas!)

As the sun sets and rapids rush headlong over the rocks below, a sprite in a soiled skirt scurries under a low archway in the stone banister. In search of scraps of food and reusable plastic strewn on the hillside she squats on the ground picking leftover fragments of cotton candy from a stick and stuffing them into her smudged little cheeks. She doesn't see me watching her as she rises and scurries under the banister to rejoin her mother holding a tattered sack.

My next stop is the sleepy Bolivian town of Copacabana on the southern shore of Lake Titicaca. I check into my cozy hilltop pad and waste no time walking into the womb of the Inca world. I catch a small craft to carry me across the lake to Isla de Sol where I trek on a pre-Columbian stone stairway to the fountain of eternal youth and commune with the spirits of Pillkugaima. I trek with Aymara and Quechua spirits across this mystical island while llama and alpaca graze on the hills and lope over the solar horizon.

Tossing Smooth Stones

Standing on the shore
of Lake Titicaca
tossing smooth stones
into cool sapphire
watching them sink slowly
into womb of Inca nation

Back in Copacabana, I stroll over to a café and order a *mate coca* to revive my spirits in the thin air of El Altiplano. After standing and stretching I wander up the narrow cobblestone streets to my crib in the sky and dream of Inca heaven.

The next morning I attend mass at the Moorish-style cathedral and offer a prayer of thanksgiving before the wood-carved Virgen de Copacabana for bringing me safely here.

Returning to Peru, my caravan to Cusco is halted by a blockade of boulders placed on the main road by angry Aymaras protesting government policies that leave them unemployed and hungry. A sturdy maternal woman wearing a derby with a red feather is perched on a boulder in the road knitting a wool scarf as she defends the cause against angry drivers whose trucks and buses are backed up by the roadblock. After an hour of confrontation and disputation between drivers and protestors, enough stones are removed from the road to permit us to move on.

Crowds of pilgrims gather on the granite high ground overlooking Sacsayhuaman on a grey rainy day to witness Inti Raymi, the ancient Incan rites and rituals in worship of the Sun and the Winter solstice. The heavens weep over Cusco as the solemn procession begins with the blowing of *conchas*, then the "Boom Boom Boom," of ceremonial drums. Then wooden flutes begin to play and legions of colorfully clad Inca soldiers, priests, vestal virgins and nobles file down from the opposite hillside onto the sacred plain; they solemnly process around the elevated sanctuary in center field.

Next the Inca's principal wife attired in white, is carried by soldiers to her royal seat in the sanctuary. Finally, with great fanfare the Incan king on his golden throne holding his golden scepter is borne by soldiers to the sanctuary where he presides over the centuries-old ceremony. The king's head is shielded from the rain by a muscular servant holding a condor-plumed umbrella. The sacred rites are performed and prayers are recited in Quechua as hundreds of maidens dance around the stage while on the surrounding hillside a kaleidoscope of banners wave in unison to the beat of the drums.

After the sacrifice of a holy llama, her flesh is carried by the high priest to the sacred bonfire where it is offered to Hanang Pacha. As the smoke rises, the condors fly skyward and the grey clouds part. The golden sun shines on a rainbow arcing over Cusco in honor of El Inca.

Now I am prepared for my spiritual trek to the sacred religious site of Machu Picchu, fifty miles from Cusco. After climbing Mt. Machu Picchu, from the summit I marvel at the ruins of Inca architecture. Polished dry stone, cut to fit together without mortar. I tread the sacred turf of the Inca and commune with their spirits at the Intihuatana: The Temple of the Sun with its two trapezoid-formed windows, with carved prominences in their four extremes, The Temple of the Three Windows with its rock formation of the neck and the head of a lama, The Temple of the Condor that honors the sacred condor who could carry souls from the land to the infinite. The Temples are dedicated to Inti, the Inca sun god and greatest deity. Standing serenely on the summit of the Inca Empire I know why Machu Picchu was voted one of the New Seven Wonders of the World.

Huanchaco

Waves at sundown are breaking sideways
along the sandy coastline
lapping up the darkened beach
where flickering torches
illuminate slender totoras
awaiting sunrise and the open sea

Laughing chattering children parade
by in colored cardboard masks
celebrating their ancestral spirits
as bonfires flicker and night falls
over the sleeping village of Huanchaco

Bohemian Holiday

Catacombas

In a Lisboa Jazz bar around midnight on Rua da Rosa
I'm talking to Marcos, the twenty something seminarian
who tells me about his secret love affair
with what he gleefully calls
"The Devil's music"

In black and white photos behind the bar
back in the day Robert Nighthawk plays
his slide guitar on Maxwell St in Chicago
and to his left Muddy Waters, eyes shut
strummin' his guitar and hummin'

On the opposite wall there's Miles
caressing his charismatic horn
and in a dusty gold frame, Lady Day
face and necklace aglow
in Satchmo's shining trumpet

A million miles from home I grin and shake my head
while sincere, celibate Marcos belts out
"Crossroads Blues" and the Spirit takes us
back to the Mississippi Delta where the blues was born
and black folks were crucified on the cross of king cotton

Then he pulls out his B-flat-harp and it's Memphis
St. Louis, Kansas City, and Chicago
Christ, am I really in Bairro Alto
diggin' the blues in candlelight?

In the back, in the dim light of Moorish lamps
two ladies in black strapless fado dresses
are sippin' and shakin' their shapely derrières

while high up, under glass Diz in that black beret
stands one foot crossing the other on tiptoe
his back arched blissfully wailing
cradling his horn

Rendezvous with Benito

Tunneling my way through Tuscany's
fields of freshly cut rolls of golden wheat
rows of corn and flocks of sheep
pass by my open window
on the second class train from Milano
to Orvieto where I rendezvous with Benito's
forlorn spirit in his family's former villa
in the Umbrian countryside where lady Lisa
wearing her short skirts and leather boots
lives with her big black dog and cats

At midnight
she tells me about her life and loves
before I slumber in the cellar
on a king size bed with Madonna smiling
down on me from the ledge on the stone wall
as fallen angels dance in my sleep

How was I to know that she is tormented
by demons from her childhood in foster homes
or that her prince charming is a pathetic drunk
whom we visit in his hilltop castle in Giovi

After downing mussels and white wine
she embraces Enzo in his dungeon
as I celebrate Festival il Sole la Luna in the village
diggin' Moroccan drums and guitar
performed in the glow of the piazza

When I return she rushes down to meet me
her tears and blood flowing
like vintage wine onto the stone stairway
where romance is scattered with the broken glass
Ignoring my advice she returns to her fate
in the midnight hour I ride home alone

Kaoutar

We meet at an outdoor market
in the middle of melancholy Amsterdam
I'm scanning the fresh fruit
when you spot me spotting you
wearing a short skirt and blouse
We walk along a canal to East of Eden
where we sip mint tea and talk
about you, a Dutch-born Moroccan

After I order water and wine you ask
"Are there many people like me in San Diego?"
"There are many Somali and Sudanese"
        I reply
"Somalis and Sudanese are not Arabs!"
        You retort—
"Neither are you!" I reply
"You're an African not an Arab—
and after 9-11 and the war on terror
Arabs are not very popular"

You search my eyes, puzzled, as
I explain how
I am proud of my African ancestry

As clouds gather over the Troppen museum
I try to explain the One Drop rule.
You don't understand how a brown brother
like me could be Black.

As day darkens and rain falls you say you love
the Dutch Antilles and have a Black boyfriend there
your sable eyes sparkle when you whisper
"Tomás I like bad boys"

Foolishly I ask—
"When you look into my eyes
what do you see?"

"You have innocence in your eyes"
  she says smiling
"But you're not a saint"

So much for romance

To Leonard Cohen

*It's spring and Greece is like a patient slowly recovering from
the colonel's junta, breathing again the fresh air of freedom.*

*Sailing into Hydra's arcing harbor at midday I meander in
the Socratic archipelago of the mind until stepping foot onto
the ground of being.*

*In a stream of sunlight I hike from the waterfront up the
stone pathway past pastel cottages, leading to a villa nesting
on the Island's western slope.*

*In the morning over breakfast my muse asks if I would like to
meet you. "Yes...yes...I want to meet the man who sang,*
Suzanne takes my hand..."

*After a short walk down the path to your wood-framed home
by the harbor with its sail boats and yachts, I rap
on your door.*

*Beautiful brunette Suzanne greets me with a smile and
invites me in. She serves "tea and oranges that come all the
way from China."*

*Then you appear, serenely smiling in your dapper linen shirt
and slacks and ask me why I came all this way.*

*"I'm a poet and I revere you and your words and music."
You glow with gratitude as we share coffee and conversation.*

*We descend to your study, a small windowless room with a
wooden chair, table, typewriter and a cot in the corner
looking out on an olive grove.*

You turn on the record player and we listen to Miles'
Sketches of Spain. We talk poetry and you give me this
advice,

"The only way to make a living from poetry is by singing it."
How easy for you to say. You create lyrical lines and carry a
tune.

When it's time to go I hand you my poems wrapped in red
ribbon; hoping and praying you will read them.

Leonard and Suzanne stand together in the open doorway
smiling as I walk to the harbor and dine on fresh fish and
down retsina.

At twilight as I sit at a café on the waterfront sipping ouzo a
contact lens falls from my eye onto the stone patio. In
distress I fall on my knees.

Then you appear and ask, "Why are you on your knees? Are
you praying?" "No, I'm looking for my lens." You focus on the
ground. Then you point down.

Following the trajectory of your slender finger I find my
missing lens. Your vision has restored my sight. Hallelujah!
Hallelujah!

After sundown I hear a knock on the mahogany door. A
poet's pilgrim is standing there. She wants to know if
Leonard Cohen is living here

Instead of inviting her in and offering her ouzo, I say, "Sorry,
Leonard Cohen isn't here; he lives down by the harbor."

She smiles, says thank you, and disappears into the night.
I wonder if she found her way to your home by the bay.

A year later I see you in Hollywood beaming like Buddha.
Phil Spector is producing your album, Death of a Ladies Man.

When I see you on the cover sitting between Suzanne and a
pilgrim in a Greek café, the sadness in your lovers' eyes say it all.

Poema Andalusia

I Pass green olive groves
and saffron fields
casas of stucco and stone
into Lorca's Andalusia of tears

Ancient land of oil lamps and grief
where Moors built the Alhambra
with sculpted rock and Koranic calligraphy
Averroes and Maimonides embraced
Aristotelian logic and reason

Gypsy, Moor and Sephardi
created Spanish soul music
           Cante Jondo
The flaming flamenco survived
la Reconquista's dagger in the heart
the auto-da-fe and Franco's Guardia Civil
Gothic cathedrals and churches built
on the blood and bones
of desecrated mosques and synagogues

Will we ever wipe away Lorca's tears
and the Prince of Peace restore
the Andalusian Spring
to Abraham's warring tribes?

Stateside in Solitude

Weekend in San Francisco

i

I cruise highway 101 through the golden hills and valleys
of Salinas and Monterey, Steinbeck's "Pastures of Heaven"
past aqueducts, rows of cotton and grapes growing on vines

I meet my old friend Shannon in Palo Alto at sunset
She's the princess of Silicon Valley who swings
her sensuous hips and flaming hair
enchanting unemployed techies
wearing software t-shirts

ii

I arrive in coastal Pacifica in time to witness
la Madonna breast feeding her bambina
while Joseph tends his cosmic crop

After years alone I nurture
a tiny pulsing miracle of flesh and blood
Whose heart beats a rhythm of hope
in a time of discord and war

Despair creeps in at dusk with deep fog
blurring a sinister street sign warning
of steep fines and towing

iii

Midday on a sunlit sidewalk in the Mission
a surrealistic stranger feeds my meter
and joins me on a tour of the City

Where we navigate crowded streets
down Market and up Columbus

95

Gleefully we greet the Beat Spirits at City Lights
Allen Ginsberg, Jack Kerouac and Bob Kaufman

At sunset window gazing strangers stroll
up Grant St. to the Afghani rug shop across from Tivoli
where girls in colored tayrans in tribal dance
as charming Abdullah plays his tablaand armonia
She leaves me to join his harem in a trance
of undulating bellies, hips, and ruby lips

I walk to Vesuvios, pour red wine on my wounds
while communing with Ferlingetti's muse
and travel home on the Bohemian Highway

Babylon by the Bay

I'm strollin' Babylon by the Bay
in North Beach when the storm
swamps the Bay Bridge
blowing down trees on Telegraph Ave.

Treasure Island is underwater and
Alcatraz is sinking in surf
The sign on the de Young museum
reads "closed due to inclement weather"

A streetcar is stuck on Nob Hill
The strip joints and bars
are nearly empty on Broadway
Lunch is canceled in Chinatown

While the mayor is getting toasted
at Town Hall I'm groovin' with Billy & Buddha
in the Old Shanghai where Jazz is still alive
on Steward Street in San Francisco

North Beach

i

I'm out on a limb in North Beach
in Café Trieste sitting beside a baby
in a bassinet as her daddy pours
over the business section of the NYT

I'm sitting where Bob Kaufman once sat
staring starry-eyed out the big bay window
through his prism of angelic vision
as he walks by on his way to café Tivoli
to sip a cappuccino and write a line

ii

I celebrate Fourth of July in Golden Gate Park
with Traci's toe nails painted red white and blue
her bust bursting blouse is patriotic too
"I'm Irish and French Canadian, she says
We make drunken lovers"

iii

She leaves me with my fears and frustrations
written on a napkin in a café on Columbus Ave.

The encounter of two souls who
knew each other in the past
and meet again
for reasons unknown
in this interval
in infinity

iv

What do I think of my ex-con old friend
and his blond-haired blue-eyed girlfriend
who listens to his late night cocaine lectures
then ponders the meaning of love in daylight
while seeking wisdom in the words of old men
walking aimlessly in empty hallways of run-down
hotels in San Francisco's North Beach

Palm Sunday

i

On Palm Sunday in Holy Week
I ride the A train uptown to St. John the Divine
looming over Harlem
where liturgy is divinely rendered by a bishop
wearing a purple zucchetto
and pita bread replaces the wafer
falling in crumbs to the cold
concrete floor
I stoop to pick up the pale fragments
of His broken body offered as sacrifice
of praise and thanksgiving for us careless
caretakers of the Holy Mystery

ii

As hard rain falls on Manhattan at midnight
lady artist, Jesse, poet David Henderson
and I break bread and drink wine together
in ecstatic conversation celebrating
the Word made flesh
on Sunday night in Mekka on Avenue A

In the Bosom of the Big Apple

*Nuyorican Poet's café in the East Village Taco Shop Poets talk
shit with a funky rhythm section that sweeps the soul of San
Diego onto the streets jammin' with lovers of the word
crammed to the rafters of the loft space shakin' to the rhythm
of the root people on East 3rd St. between Ave. B & C where
Latino New Yorkers live and die on concrete in the Big Apple
as rhyme and rhythm converge in the bosom of the big mango I
emerge from underground like Kafka lost in the wet windswept
city searching for a place to flop for the night until dawn and
then drift across Central Park at daybreak until I reach the
museum mile: the millennium art show at the Whitney, the
Met's monster collection with prophet John Brown raging like
Moses against slavery whose fierce will fortifies me for the street*

Suzanne

*You are like a simple melody
the seductive strains of which
being mortal, I cannot resist
I miss the warm caress of your smile
but I shall wait awhile
perhaps forever—
To have another vision
of your face and figure
it's your decision—
I spied a question in your eyes
the place where truth resides
The answer was provided
but I was not confided
thus I try in vain
to drive your memory
from my brain—
To no avail
would my will prevail*

and in response to your
wall of silence
I have written this verse
in defiance
Suzanne, this is not a mere
love letter
I hope it is something better—
For these sentiments I extol
are buried deep within my soul

Meditation on Middle Age

A middle-aged man sits alone
in a small café in San Diego
sipping his Moroccan mint as he peers
out the window at the intersection
of 30th and Beech Street
trippin' on Miles soulful sound
soaring through the open door
to the rhythm of the street

"So What" is Miles lyrical reply to
those who wonder why a middle-aged man
sits alone at a small café with pen in hand
sipping mint tea on a rainy day

Alone Together

At Rebecca's café on Sunday afternoon
watching young and old walk in
with their lifeline laptops
 iPads and iPhones
order coffee, tea and scones
then plug into and turn on the web
to blog, to text, to tweet
to live in virtual reality

No polite or heated conversation
on the loss of life in the war on terror
and the loss of liberty at home

Today we come together at Rebecca's
to be alone with each other in cyberspace

South Park Blues

It's Saturday night in South Park and the blues is blastin'
from the stage of the Bar & Grill to the street where we
celebrate and dance the blues away in the wailing of bass,
guitar, sax, harp and strokin' sticks and brushes

Taking me back to where my grandpapi and the blues were
born in Mississippi Delta moonshine where the cotton fields
calloused his hands and where my granduncle's blood flowed
in Mississippi mud

Isabel is serving food and drinks in her skin tight blue jeans
blissin' and blessin' from behind as I sip my wine and scratch
a line on a piece of paper searching for love in rhythm and
rhyme

As the night wears on strains from the sax stream across the
street into my backseat as I ride home alone with the blues
serenading me I turn off the lights and dream of Isabel's
divine derriere

Take me back to where my grandpapi and the blues were
born in Mississippi Delta moonshine where the cotton fields
calloused his hands and where granduncle's blood flowed in
Mississippi mud

Take me back to where Grandpapi and the blues were born
take me back
        take me back
            take me back!

Bass Player
(for Evona Wascinski)

She straddles the bass like her lover
her slender fingers stroking
the strands
up and down
down and up

Her right thigh pumping
eyes closed thumping
plucking a funky beat
that throbs
and thrills

Then cleaves the heart
her slender fingers stroking
the strands
up and down
down and up

She and her bass
crescendo in climax
of rhythm and blues
du dum da dum dum
du dum da dum dum dum

Jim and Andy's After Hours

Dining at the Red Fox with my old friend
Ann Williams as the piano player serenades
us with one of our favorites, Body and Soul

Ann is an adopted child who grew up on a farm
in Mt. Vernon, Ohio, "Where they have a big sign
saying 'Home of Daniel Emmett who wrote Dixie'"

She tells me about her life in the Big Apple
as a Jazz singer in the early sixties
hangin' out with Jazz stars and sidemen

at Jim and Andy's on 48th and 6th Ave.
after the clubs closed and the luminaries
of Jazz gathered to jam with the jukebox

How Gerry Mulligan pressed her against the wall
whispering in her ear, "Your album cover should
be above mine and I should be on top of you."

How one evening while dining and drinking
Lena leaned over and whispered in her ear
"Would you like to have an affair?"

And the night Sarah Vaughn arrived after
singing at Basin Street East and Ann told her
"You gave me the thrill of my life tonight

You are the nearest thing to singing like an angel
I have ever heard." Sarah stood up and said
"Oh shit!" and walked out onto Broadway

I'm Diggin'

in the Summer heat
the Congolese beat
                    beat
                            beat
of the talking drum
and the Choctaw Cherokee
tom
        tom
                tom

I'm a native son
dancin' on soul street
to the beat
                beat
                        beat

of the talking drum
and the Choctaw Cherokee
tom
        tom
                tom

The big dipper & half moon
glow as the urban rivers flow
to the beat
                beat
                        beat

of the talking drum
and the Choctaw Cherokee
tom
        tom
                tom

Dig it!

Pass it On

It's springtime in Seattle
and the sun is shining
when I arrive at Sea Tac
without any change
in my pocket
The bus driver says
"Come on!"

I sit next to a guy
wearing a baseball cap
and a Mariners' windbreaker
who hands me the fare
and says
"Pass it on."

The tulips and cherry blossoms
are in blazing bloom
the Lake is gleaming
lovely ladies are beaming
as I leisurely stroll
the sunny streets
of Seattle in springtime

Pass it on

In a Wilderness

In a wilderness
of wood wind water and ice
freed from the concrete
plastic prison
soiled air and water
killing king salmon
melting Arctic ice
habitat of perishing polar bears

I'm alone
arms raised in awe
to grizzlies
caribou and wolves
who roam over mountains
glaciers and razored ridges
rising from rocky river beds
and silt layered flatlands

In a wilderness of wood wind
water and ice I tread
on a carpet of moss and lichen
where water flows and falls
in a woodland harmony
of cottonwood
ferns, alder and sitka Spruce
beneath a soaring eagle eye

Creepin' In the Canyon

One day in North Park
like a lost coyote
crossing a rocky river bed—
then climbing a steep slope
of blossoming daffodils
until reaching Montclair Park—
where los Mexicanos
ballet with soccer balls
and unleashed dogs bark
as black birds dance
across the sparkling sky

Borrego Blues

We flee the city's cyber cafés & cell phones
for the silence of dry river beds
moonshine and jackrabbits

We trudge through thickets
that scourge the skin
ascending rocky riverbeds
to the canyon wall
where pristine
silence sets the soul on fire
as ribbons of sky blue satin
ripple like cresting waves

We set our tent on primal sand
as light fades on crayon hills
the smiling moon spreads
a blanket of stardust
over slumbering
intruders in the night

107

On Retreat

Alone with myself
and the Prince of Peace
in chapel—
monks in choir
wearing black
ample hoods
scapulars
and wide black belts
one end hanging
from a buckle
cinched at the side
chanting the offices—
Opus Dei, the work of God
before sunrise
until sunset
in rhythm with the hours
and the seasons

After vespers
alone in my drafty cell
I search the dark night
of the soul—
peering onto a patch of pavement
lit by a lonely lamppost
before a chapel door
where the black Madonna
delivers me from
self pity
to her suffering Son

Author Biography

Tomás was born and raised in Seattle, Washington, the grandson of African American pioneers. He began writing verse soon after graduating with a Juris Doctor from the University of Washington. Tomás is a Civil Rights attorney/activist and world traveler who lives in San Diego. His poetry is his life in verse.

His words appear in various publications and literary journals. Tomás' most recent volume of poetry is *Vientos de Cambio/ Winds of Change*, published by *Poetic Matrix Press*. Others include: *Yazoo City Blues, Time of the Poet, Dark Symphony in Duet* with the late Sarah Fabio, and *Two Races, One Face*, with John Peterson. Tomas' work is also featured on his website (www.sambajia.com).

CPSIA information can be obtained at www.ICGtesting.com
Printed in the USA
BVOW020523120313

315282BV00001B/1/P